A CAREER IN
ACCOUNTANCY

A CAREER IN ACCOUNTANCY

Garth Pedler

Matador
9 Priory Business Park,
Wistow Road, Kibworth Beauchamp,
Leicestershire LE8 0RX
Tel: 0116 279 2299
Email: books@troubador.co.uk
Web: www.troubador.co.uk/matador
Twitter: @matadorbooks

ISBN 978 1788032 865

British Library Cataloguing in Publication Data.
A catalogue record for this book is available from the British Library.

Printed and bound by CPI Group (UK) Ltd, Croydon, CR0 4YY
Typeset in 11pt Garamond by Troubador Publishing Ltd, Leicester, UK

Matador is an imprint of Troubador Publishing Ltd

This book is dedicated to the memory of John Frederick Palmer of Cuffley who wound me up and left me ticking and counting for half a century.

CONTENTS

Part One   1

Early Years

Part Two   8

I Enter the City

Part Three   54

While Working at James Goldsmith

Part Four   74

Working Entirely on My Own

Part Five   115

Kibblewhite versus Commissioners of Inland Revenue

Part Six   123

Forced Retirement

PART ONE

EARLY YEARS

I HAVE JUST HAD to retire as a result of failed eye surgery and had to dispose of my long-established accountancy practice. I have now come to grips with the sudden change in my life and found myself quietly reflecting on what has been a very comfortable, stress-free career in accountancy.

I had not considered my future career until I came home from boarding school for the Easter 1963 holidays and my mother asked, "Has Mr Harvey discussed what career you might wish to pursue?" Mr Harvey was my housemaster and also taught us French. He was often on sick leave with what transpired to be throat cancer, so he seldom saw us boys. I replied that we had not even discussed back in autumn 1961 what A-level subject I should be studying, let alone talked about some suitable career for me. As I seemed to do rather well with mathematics and enjoyed figures generally, I muttered that I had been thinking of becoming a chartered accountant. We left it at that. Mother could have telephoned the headmaster to ask why these important topics had been overlooked, but she did not do so.

It was always my mother who made the decisions in our Cardiff household. She had trained as a hairdresser and also dabbled in retail drapery when living in Newton Abbot. In 1933 her father, who was a railwayman, was promoted to locomotive foreman at Exeter St David's depot. This necessitated a change of family home to Exeter. Briefly her parents bought the freehold of a house near Cowick Street with unpleasant neighbours, so they moved to a 'new-build' at Blenheim Road in nearby Alphington. A certain Thomas Pedler's parents had also bought one of these new houses and he and my mother immediately became Blenheim

Road's first romance and were duly wedded by Parson Bennett in Alphington church in 1937.

My father had been to Hele's Grammar School in Exeter, and had become a works chemist with the Exeter Gas, Light & Coke Company. When war broke out in 1939 this was a 'Reserve Status Employment' so he could not be conscripted. However, in 1940 he became restless and obtained permission to volunteer for the British army. Here, the recruiting officer directed him to one of Mr Churchill's secret establishments, which was a chemical warfare research unit within the Royal Engineers. After some months Mr Churchill decided we were not going to have a chemical war. The unit disbanded and Father and his colleagues were transferred into another unit newly established to research radar. It has always puzzled me that the powers that be should think that chemists can easily become physicists. My father was one of those men who did not understand physics let alone radar so he was quite at a loose end. However, when he returned to civilian life in 1946 he was in no way the gallant young man that he had been when he had married before the war. It would appear that during his service something must have damaged Father's health because on his return from the war it appeared his thyroid was seriously harmed by a chemical experiment. In those days such problems were seldom correctly diagnosed but if they were, the treatments available were often unreliable. It was not an unusual situation and there were many people like him whose similar symptoms first appeared in adulthood. In accordance with government directives, he had to be given back his old employment at the Exeter Gas, Light & Coke Co. He would now be the last into the office each morning, after my mother had chivvied him into rising, and the last home each evening, having been chased out of the office by the caretaker. I am sure he would not have held down the employment for long but, fortuitously, in a zealous moment the new Labour government nationalised the nation's entire miscellany of Gas, Light & Coke companies as the new Ministry of Fuel & Power.

The Ministry decreed that its local office for Wales and the

South-West of England was to be at 27 Newport Road, Cardiff while they were building a new E-shaped block of government offices in the suburb of Gabalfa. Father had to be based in Cardiff so this necessitated our moving as a family from our ancestral Devon to Cardiff, where Mother managed to find a house on the main road to Caerphilly and she resumed her hairdressing business.

After a few weeks a delivery van arrived outside the house and two men started unloading a fridge. Mother had not ordered a fridge. It was extremely difficult to buy one in the years immediately after the war but she kept her cool when she realised that the delivery label said Peglers of Caerphilly. Now Peglers were grocers throughout South Wales and had a branch in the town of Caerphilly. Mother realised a very fortuitous error had occurred and during the lunch hour took the necessary cash demanded on the accompanying invoice to the distributor's warehouse in the city centre and obtained the receipt. Pegler's discovered the mistake too late and had to wait quite some time for another fridge to be delivered while we could hardly believe our luck.

To our great relief we discovered that once you had a job in the Civil Service it was a job for life and in those days you could not be retired before the age of 65 (ladies aged 60) unless you committed some dreadful misdemeanour. Therefore, as Father had a secure job but no prospects of promotion, Mother used the profits of her hairdressing business to send me three years later to Llandaff Cathedral Preparatory School.

The school's headmaster was Mr Norman Westbury-Jones and he had in his care 129 young pupils. Mrs Westbury-Jones acted as the secretary and bursar. On more than one occasion she had to telephone my father at work to remind him that the school closed at 13:00hrs on Saturdays, and the pupils needed to be collected promptly. Even now I recall telling her week after week that Dad's office telephone number was Cardiff 9234.

I had been at the school for almost six years and was thoroughly enjoying it when apparently Mr Westbury-Jones told Mother that I was showing antagonistic traits. He was well aware that she was at her wits' end trying to get Father out of bed and off to work each day. She would be shouting loudly at him when most mothers would be just preparing their children for school. Recognising the situation, Mr Westbury-Jones suggested that I might be better off in an easier and calmer environment and proposed that a boarding school might be a good idea. Mother asked some of the parents of boys who had recently left about the schools to which their sons had passed on reaching the age of 13. Some of the parents were her hairdressing clients. In those days public school headmasters did not perform such ambassadorial duties as they do nowadays in visiting prospective parents at prep school symposiums, and therefore my mother took Mr. Westbury-Jones' advice and contacted a couple of possible schools in the West Country. It was decided that we should consider some schools between Cardiff and Exeter, where our relatives still lived.

Mr Westbury-Jones had noticed that Father's handwriting was probably the neatest that he had ever read but Mother's, while firm and resolute, was rather illegible. The headmaster politely recommended that Father should write the letters. Accordingly they wrote to Clifton College at Bristol. That school replied that there were no vacancies in my age group. However, the headmaster of King's College Taunton, Mr Randall Unmack, replied that he did have a vacancy 'due to the Suez Crisis'. He had lately acquired a new campus for his preparatory school, for which he was recruiting new pupils. It was a fine Georgian country house named Pyrland Hall. Mr Westbury-Jones had sent details of my academic prowess to Mr Unmack who invited us to visit his preparatory and senior schools.

One day during the summer holidays Mother and I took the train to Taunton and Mr Unmack showed us around the substantial senior school building. It had been erected in 1867 and displayed an ornate Gothic Victorian façade. My abiding memory was his flinging open an upstairs door to reveal two long rows of thirty-eight steel bedsteads, neatly dressed with emerald green blankets. We then drove in his extraordinary Ford V8 Pilot car at terrifying speed through the centre of Taunton to Pyrland Hall, the preparatory school just north of the town. Built by Sir William Yea in 1757, it was situated on the southern slopes of the Quantock Hills with fine views across the Vale of Taunton Deane to the distant Blackdown Hills; its master-in-charge was Mr Andrew Shawyer. The classic Georgian house had a magnificent stone portico and some of the rooms were finely proportioned with very high ceilings. Its estate had been reduced to eight acres of grounds with small woodlands around three sides, certainly enough space for us boys to enjoy our free time to the full.

For centuries, the landed gentry in Britain had employed servants in their houses and on their estates. Legislation introduced around 1904 established schools for the working classes on whom the estates had depended for their labourers. Many of the sons of the gentry were killed in action in the First World War along with several of their staff who had also taken up arms. After the war many of the large country houses were abandoned for want of family heirs or their servants. Servicemen returning from the war were able to get jobs by virtue of their education and were less eager to enter service at the grand houses. A similar situation occurred when the nation emerged from the Second World War. More and more large houses of the gentry became available for use as schools, hotels, health spas, etc.

The last private owner of Pyrland Hall had been a Colonel Pemberton, who had bought it on his retirement from the army in 1911. During the Second World War it was requisitioned for army headquarters but, being a loyal retired officer, he was allowed to continue to reside in three of the rooms. Certainly nobody else would have understood the intricacies of all the drains, the fuse boxes, the eccentric plumbing arrangements and the quirks of the heating system.

Pyrland Hall was therefore one of the few country houses lucky enough to have been maintained in an exceptionally good state of repair throughout the war while entirely used by the Army.

After the Colonel died at a great age in 1950 his niece at once sold the property at auction. King's College bought the reduced estate and the National Trust bought much of the rest of the surrounding estate. I thoroughly enjoyed the combination of my education and playing in the surrounding woodlands at Pyrland Hall.

In 1959 I won a small scholarship to the senior school where the prospectus assured the parents that their children would receive careers advice, but the master who had been assigned the task had also been solely responsible for the school's geography syllabus and the rest of his time was spent as a sports referee and assistant housemaster. In my final summer term in 1964, the headmaster sent him around the school with a clipboard and instructions to see each of the pupils then leaving and to ask what career they intended to pursue. Eagerly I waited my turn to have a chat with him. When he found me by the geography department stairs I told him that I was thinking of becoming a chartered accountant. I had a view to go into business management and I asked if he could give me some advice. He glanced at his watch, muttered that the school was breaking up at the end of the week, and I never heard from him again.

In 1960 our house in Cardiff had a shop beyond the front door on the former front garden. It also embraced the former front room whose door still opened into the front door corridor. One day as I was running towards the former front door my mother opened the door of the front room which had been re-hung to swing into the corridor, thereby giving her more space in the room for her hairdressing business. I ran straight into this door as it was opening and must have suffered concussion. Never again was I the bright lad who had won that scholarship.

After my accident I gradually fell behind in my schoolwork and failed to gain a place at Oxbridge or even Southampton or Bristol Universities.

In 1962 the Civil Service transferred Father's job from Gabalfa in Cardiff to Holborn in central London and we moved to the village of Datchet, situated west of London by the River Thames. My father's job in Holborn was on a pay scale sufficient to run a home, a car, a one-child family, and only a small portion of my school fees, the rest of which my mother afforded from the sale of her hairdressing business in Cardiff. My mother did not resume business in Datchet, largely because she had to look after her widowed father.

My mother had a first cousin, Yvonne, who had married a musician. They had emigrated in the 1930s to live in New Zealand and in 1951 Yvonne returned to visit the family in Devon. I met her then in Exeter and my mother maintained correspondence with her abroad. In 1963 Yvonne came over once again. My mother had written to her that I had been thinking of becoming a chartered accountant and also realised that I had a penchant for recasting inefficient railway branch line timetables. However, the family felt that I could not risk seeking a job with British Railways after the transport minister, Mr Ernest Marples, had told Dr Beeching to close down vast tracts of the railway system.

Yvonne had once worked as a secretary for the small firm of chartered accountants named B. de V. Hardcastle, Burton & Co. in the City of London. She had married in 1928, at a time when women had to resign from employment upon marrying. She had kept in touch with her former boss, Mr Arthur Palmer, by exchange of Christmas cards so she wrote to tell him about me. My mother asked my father to write a follow-up letter in his impeccable handwriting for an interview with the company. As a result, I was invited to an interview with the company later that year.

PART TWO

I ENTER THE CITY

FOLLOWING MY FINAL Summer Term at Taunton in 1964, I went
on the school's Corps Camp. On my return home to Datchet,
my father whisked me off to Hardcastle's offices at 3, South Place,
near Broad Street Station. We found it was still a very small firm.
There, the elderly senior partner, Mr Arthur Palmer, Yvonne's old
employer, met us and showed us into his son John's room, where
we were given tea and talked about my becoming an articled clerk
in the firm.

During this introductory interview I was pleased to learn
that I would be carefully guided into the profession and helped
to take the appropriate exams. This would be done through the
accountancy tutorial institution named H. Foulkes Lynch & Co.
Ltd. It was recommended that I buy a correspondence course to
study at home. To be truthful I found it worthwhile and it was
easy to keep to their rigid schedules. The entire course cost £52,
of which Buckinghamshire County Council refunded £39. This
was to be my one and only educational grant.

In Mr Arthur Palmer's day the clerks had had to pay to be
articled but the profession had moved on and by 1964 all of its
trainees were paid small salaries. As an articled clerk my salary
was to start at £250 per annum, which adequately covered the
remarkably cheap annual rail season ticket from Datchet to
Waterloo, and I could also look forward to periodic increases. We
signed all of the indenture papers and I was told that I could begin
work as soon as I wished. We set a date of three weeks ahead.

On our way home my father bought me the first of these rail
season tickets. I would of course have to pay for all of the future
ones out of my own salary. Father also bought me a smart grey

suit and tie, as Mr Palmer had directed. The office hours were from 09.00 hrs to 17.00 hrs and I presented myself promptly on the agreed Monday morning. I was greeted by the secretary who was doing the job that cousin Yvonne had done so many years earlier.

John Palmer led me into the clerks' room and introduced me to the senior clerk, Alan Phillips, seated near the door, and then to a very quiet humble clerk named Frank Green across the room. Alan told me that we must always address the partners as Mr Arthur and Mr John. Mr John enquired as to the whereabouts of the only other clerk, Mike Griffiths. Alan told him that he would be late as he was delivering a parcel to clients. Mr John protested that Mike had already undertaken that task on the previous Friday evening and left the room in some dismay. I would never work with Mr Arthur as he always handed down any of the tasks which needed clerical assistance to his son. Our office negotiations with the Inland Revenue were left entirely to Mr John. Not one of the clerks was ever directly involved in answering the Revenue's questions.

Our suite of four offices was on the first floor at the front of the building. The first room was next to the open steel-framed lift. One had to open and shut the steel concertina gates, which always made a clatter, and be careful not to catch one's fingers. Mr John told me never to let clients try to open or close the gates on their own. I cannot ever remember the lift breaking down. I recall that the stairs around the lift and all of the adjacent corridors were formed in a mass of Edwardian marble. It was all 'period', like the building. The arrangement of our rooms, all of which were painted in a light drab grey, like the corridor and stairs, was practical and satisfactory. The first office in the suite was the largest and was occupied by the clerks. The firm's entire filing system was in cabinets down each side of the room. In the middle was one wide, long table capable of accommodating three clerks on each side. Their heaps of files were set down the middle when required. Mr Arthur was very insistent that we never have more files than necessary on the table. The top of this table was inset with leather moquette, the edges of which were gilded with a simple design. As there were never more than four clerks we always had adequate space. I could not understand why other accountancy firms had smaller tables for their staff.

The second office was that of the one and only secretary. It had two connecting doors, one into our room and one on the opposite side into Mr Arthur's office. His office had a further door into Mr John's office which was at the end of our corridor. We were not allowed to pass through Mr Arthur's office to reach Mr. John's so would always have to walk along the corridor when needed, past the two other offices to Mr John's office. Meetings with clients and AGMs would always be held in Mr Arthur's office, which was larger than either Mr John's or the secretary's.

One afternoon every week, Mr Arthur used to play golf near his home in Hertfordshire. In his place came Beevor de Vere-Hardcastle, the founder of the firm. He had been born in 1880 and was now 84. He would undertake this weekly pilgrimage to do whatever little work he still had. He would always collect the £12 cash weekly portion of his annuity that the firm was obliged to pay him which Mr Arthur had left for him in a sealed envelope.

Mr Arthur would always appear to be very reluctant to leave this annuity for Beevor, and I do not understand why. After all, without his founding the firm many decades earlier, it would not exist!

The second Mr Hardcastle, Beevor's son, ran the company's branch office in Northwood, Middlesex. I remember it was very well sited at a roundabout which, if my memory is correct, was on the busy A40. Occasionally he would bring his own clients to use Mr Arthur's room and we noticed that Mr Arthur was quite content for young Mr Hardcastle to use his room if he was away for his weekly game of golf. However, he would get irritable if Mr Hardcastle asked if he could bring a client on any other day, because he had to share Mr John's office. When the threats to his office space receded, Mr Arthur would resume his jovial character.

In my first few days with the firm Mr Arthur had finished some work and asked me to take the books back to a client in Wardour Street. Their bookkeeper would be able to bring them up to date and Mr Arthur would follow me on an hour later when the office typing was finished.

I climbed up the stairs to the reception of the Wardour Street offices and passed a door marked Bob Monkhouse. As I waited for Mr Arthur I sat in hopes of catching a glimpse of this already legendary comedian. I was to be disappointed. Our client and Mr Arthur talked for a long time while I wrote down the occasional note that they dictated to me.

In our own offices on each desk there was a large and very heavy telephone set. It enabled us to reach all of the other six extensions in the office and also to transfer calls to each other. Our clients knew that our telephone number was MONarch 5290 but secretly there was another number line to this contraption, MONarch 5367. That number was only to be used for outgoing calls and under no circumstances, Alan Phillips had emphasised, was it ever to be given to our clients.

When I tactlessly asked Alan whether he had finished his exams I found that he had not passed any, and when I put the same question to Frank Green, I got the same muted reply. To avoid more embarrassment Alan told me that Mike, whose late arrival was still eagerly awaited, had been on a crammer course in the Conway Valley for several weeks and yet even he had failed.

I was more than a little alarmed to find that I had joined a firm where the two partners were the only chartered accountants. One of them had qualified a generation before the other and in those days exams would have been very different. Alan sensed my concern and quickly reassured me that one clerk from the office had recently succeeded in qualifying. I was of course very relieved to hear that. He was Mr Tye and he would return every few months to have lunch with Mr John.

A recognised perk at most city firms were the daily luncheon vouchers given in addition to one's salary. These came in various denominations. The lowest denomination was half a crown (2s: 6d or two shillings and sixpence – nowadays 12½p), and it was free of income tax. Mr John gave us all three shillings' worth – the extra sixpence was taxable and should have been declared on tax returns. Whenever I was in the main office I would go for lunch to the Red Lion on the corner of the street where there was a small restaurant above the bar room. I invariably had the meat pie, mash and peas (they cost two shillings and eleven pence), plus fruit tart and custard at the cost of seven pence, totalling three shillings and six pence (nowadays 17½p). There was a waitress service to each table.

Alan gave me my first client task. It was to prepare a 52-line cost schedule of the weekly business of a public house, their totals being in the first column and its analysis spread over several columns. Next I had to add up (which we called casting) and then ensure that the totals of the analysis columns equalled the grand total of the first column and show it to him when I had finished. Then I had to prepare an income schedule for the same 52 weeks and usually there was only one column of weekly totals and no analysis columns. It was a rule that no member of staff was allowed to use the office's sole mechanical, lever-operated adding machine until he had worked in the firm for a whole year. We all very quickly learned to add up in our heads at great speed; it was essential to add the column downwards and then upwards to see if the sum was the same. It was a faculty for which I have always been extremely grateful to Hardcastle's. I was then shown how to make a Trial Balance using the new totals. Opening balances were brought forward from last year's Trial Balance. I would always be hugely satisfied when it all came together perfectly at the end.

Next, Alan showed me how to fill in the accounts and how to do a Balance Sheet using various rates of depreciation. When finished the papers would go to Mr John for the next stage and I repeated the processes with the books of another pub all over again. I thought that the exercise was very satisfying and quite fun.

A couple of days later Mr John called me into his office to say that he was very happy with my first task. He had booked me on to a training course for what would nowadays be termed 'wannabe' chartered accountants. Until then I passed my time doing more and more 52-line pubs and their accounts.

During three weeks each October, the Institute of Chartered Accountants ran courses at various polytechnics around the London suburbs. As I lived in Datchet my venue would be the Ealing Technical College. One peak hour train each morning went round the 'Hounslow Loop' line instead of direct to London Waterloo and I could catch a bus from Hounslow to Ealing. In fact I quickly found one other student, who drove via Hounslow, on the course and he gave me a lift to and from the station. Hardcastle's paid my extra travel costs. I felt that the Institute had designed a very appropriate course and had chosen a superb tutor. Oddly enough in the lunchtime canteen I met two other students who had lately come direct from the same school as myself and were studying other technical subjects.

Among the other students on the course was a young Stewart Liberty of the famous London department store. His later career would be no surprise to anyone. He complained vehemently of having to travel daily from Great Missenden to London Marylebone and then out from Paddington Station to Ealing.

As we were finishing this course, I received a letter through the universities' clearing system in October offering me a place to read accountancy at Southampton

University. At once I wrote thanking them and explained that I had already signed Articles to train to be a chartered accountant. When I returned to the office in the City three weeks later, Mr John asked whether I had found the course useful. I told him that our lecturer had delivered it well and enthused us all. However, there was a sore point for me. We students had discussed our salaries and I found that at £250 a year, mine was by far the lowest. Most were getting between £350 and £450 a year.

Mr John promised to have a word with Mr Arthur and a few days later he called me to his office. I was to hear that my salary would be raised to £300 a year with immediate effect and I was content. Many months later Frank told me that as a result of my request everyone else's salary also had to be raised. Mr Arthur had 'gone ballistic', telling Mr. John that he should never have sent me on the course!

In the office there was no photocopier, nor even a Gestetner duplicating machine. In those days Gestetners were mostly used in schools to prepare multiple copies of exam papers. Mr John was clearly exasperated at trying to get the firm up to date and to take it into the future.

Our office secretary would work her way through several boxes of carbon paper, being careful to type faultlessly on her heavy-duty mechanical typewriter. On the few occasions that photocopying was necessary she would go to a machine on a platform in Liverpool Street Station, which was nearby. When, on the few occasions that photocopying was necessary, I would have to go to a machine in Liverpool Street Station. However, it printed all the black text in white and all the white background in black. Photocopying was still primitive in those days!

Mr John was a member of the Honourable Artillery Company, where he held the rank of Captain. The Artillery Company's headquarters were at Armoury House in City Road. I am sure that he would meet many of our clients there and he could also be introduced to their friends as potential clients in the course of time.

One such client was Sir Murray Fox, an alderman of the City of London. He was the son of an earlier client, Sir Sidney Fox, a one-time Lord Mayor of London. Sir Murray was also in line to be the mayor in a couple of years and Mr. John was paying very special attention to his tax affairs.

Every time we walked along the Barbican, we would see Sir Murray's brand new office block of about six storeys, Murray House, which stood surrounded by cleared bombsites mostly awaiting redevelopment.

It is not generally known that unlike the recently conceived office of Mayor of (all) London, the mayors of the City traditionally spent a substantial part of their own personal fortunes whilst in office in promoting the City at home and abroad. I heard the woeful story that, at a late moment, Sir Murray realised that he would not be able to afford to become mayor and that he had to decline the honour. However, many years later I heard that he had ultimately achieved his ambition.

Back at Hardcastle's I was beginning to get a little suspicious of the plethora of 'pub jobs' that were being passed my way. They all came from the firm of J. Carroll & Sons, stock takers who visited public houses and similar establishments to record an inventory of their unsold goods. The company had old offices above Mansion House Station where I would return each pub's books and collect fresh ones. I noticed that all the records were written up in the same hand rather than by the various publicans and that the only printed documents that I ever saw were bank statements for the banking takings and for paying cheques. The daily takings would be handwritten by the same person for all 52 weeks of the year. All the books were written up in only one or two hands. Moreover, the gross profit for each pub was almost always close to 14·7%. Nowadays any accountant would be immediately alarmed to see the similarity of the books of businesses which engaged the same stock taker. Obviously I had cottoned on to something which could easily upset the Inland Revenue, but my carefully voiced concerns were brushed aside. Nowadays such accounting practices would be discouraged.

Hardcastle's City office notepaper referred to the other branches at Birchington-on-Sea in Kent and Northwood in Middlesex. None of the clerks knew anything about the staff at the other offices and would not have recognised a partner if we ever saw one other than the young Mr Hardcastle from Northwood.

Once Mr John heard that the Birchington-on-Sea office was one staff member short for doing the audit of a button factory in upmarket Upper Sydenham. He volunteered my services for three weeks and I was expected to stay with their auditors at the nearby Queen's Hotel, Sydenham. This was no great distance from the

Crystal Palace, destroyed by fire 29 years earlier. The job sounded interesting.

The two clerks from the Birchington office were affable but after dinner on the first evening, the one who was obviously in charge took out some cards and dice and invited me to play. I said that I did not gamble and I was quite disconcerted by the strength of his insistence. None of us in the City office gambled. I said that if he persisted I would go to Mr Palmer and ask not to be attached to the Birchington office again. I cannot recall whether the other man was content to gamble but the first one certainly gave up trying to entice me.

Back in the City office some time later, I was sent with Mike Griffiths to work on the books of another firm, J. Davy & Co. Ltd. It was a very long-established wine shipping company. Their head office was in John Adam Street in the Adelphi area. Adelphi was actually the name for the area before Charing Cross Station was built. Davy's, proud of their own vintage, continued to use the words 'The Adelphi' even in their telegram address. They employed as their cellar man an elderly man called Greg. He wore the obligatory light brown store coat. He was soon to retire because, in working day in, day out in the damp cellars, he had contracted a lung condition with which the company directors would not concern themselves.

The company director's office on the ground floor was something of a museum of old office equipment. It housed one of the earliest typewriters that I had ever seen. Some other piece of apparatus was standing on the mantelpiece. Mike, assuring himself that it would not be missed, took it home. However, an elderly director who had the annoying habit of calling everyone Michael spotted the theft next day and he rang Mr John. Mr John vehemently reprehended Mike for his gross misconduct and this ancient artefact was duly returned to its mantelpiece in John Adam Street the next day. On the corner of John Adam Street was an old stamp shop where I bought some cylinder blocks of King Edward VII postage stamps at prices far below those in the catalogue of

Stanley Gibbons, the famous stamp dealers, whose shop was just along the Strand. I was puzzled that other stamp collectors in the vicinity had not found this small treasure trove themselves. I think that the proprietor was unaware of their rising prices. I still have them today.

Mike's pride and joy was a vintage Lagonda motorcar of about 1928. He told us how one Saturday morning he had stopped at a zebra crossing in Cricklewood. Two elderly ladies, passing in opposite directions but with their eyes on his fine car, walked into each other. He chuckled and made the car backfire as he started away, scaring the wits out of them.

It is to another clerk, Frank Green, that I owe my enduring love of the Surrey countryside. He had just bought himself a Humber motorcar second-hand for £300 and it was in excellent order. Frank really came into his own when we were sent to audit the books of E.H. Perkins & Co. Ltd, church furnishers, on the main road close to Surbiton station. To reach their premises avoiding London, I would change trains at Staines. Frank would drive his Humber from his terraced home in the East End. His car was perhaps the pride of his East End street.

At Perkins' we worked all morning to the clattering of two wooden looms, of forgotten vintage, being operated by highly skilled weavers. They would make to order chasubles for clergymen or whatever else was required of them.

Every lunchtime we would walk out past the bookkeeper. He was middle-aged, immaculately spoken, and always dressed in a sparkling white shirt and black bow tie. He was in charge of the telephone. In those days Surbiton was the last manually operated telephone exchange, known as Elmbridge exchange. The dials on the telephones did not work but presumably were ready for the exchange to be modernised. Frank and I would have a quick and tasty meal somewhere along the parade, and then drive off into the depths of the countryside in the Humber for the rest of what was at least a two-hour-long lunch break. Without the aid of a map Frank knew all of the picturesque parts of Surrey. We never left the car but would stop briefly to see the views and then got back to Perkins' much refreshed. He had the knack of being able to convince Mr John that we needed an extra day for our work and Perkins' staff never seemed to question the number of days that our half-yearly task took us. For me it was a really pleasant experience, well away from Carroll's 'pub jobs', and Mr John never took us to task.

Twice a year I accompanied Alan Phillips on a job at South Herts Golf Club. Alan told me that a famous golfer was the resident coach there and that I might see him in the flesh. However, I was really not interested in golf or golfers.

Another biannual task with Alan was at Beckenham Working Men's Social Club. Their bookkeeper and secretary was a man who also worked at a Fleet Street newspaper each evening.

One lunchtime the three of us passed through the large bar room and heard a commotion. A fruit machine stood beyond the end of the bar and was chugging away expelling a mountain of coins. A member of the club had won the jackpot, a rare event which attracted everyone's attention. Such a payout was so seldom achieved that the barman kept a board on which he recorded these rare occasions. The surprised winner exclaimed, "I only put in three sixpences!"

We resumed our work and the secretary saw me checking the additions in the books. He asked if I would like to borrow his adding machine. Alan quickly explained that as I was in my first year I was not yet allowed to use any calculating machine. Some of Hardcastle's clients still did not use them either.

Mr John occasionally took me away to see clients with him. Once we finished too late for me to make my way home and he offered to put me up for the night at his home at Cuffley in Hertfordshire, where I was pleased to meet his charming wife, Margaret.

I recall working at Hallett, Fox & White, auctioneers and valuers in Wood Street in the City of London. Their office was on the site of the old City Compter, the debtors' prison. The firm was obliged under its building permit to allow the public access on request to view the last remaining cellar in which there were still shackles for prisoners. Presumably this is still the case.

I believe that Hallett's was a company that had once belonged to Sir Sidney Fox and had then become Sir Murray's concern. The company had an auctioneer's premises on the Old Holloway Road where an occasional customer was Honor Kaufmann, known professionally as the actress Honor Blackman. Alas, the auction house had to close in its 99th year as the business had ceased to be viable.

When in the City I would stride briskly out of the office at 17.00 hrs to Bank Station where there is a one-stop tube line to Waterloo station. The old trains had the shape of sleek grey space rockets and the service in the peak hours was frequent. The little trains were always overcrowded and affectionately known as 'the Drain'. Reaching Waterloo station, if I ran up the stairs I could catch the 17.24 hrs slam-door train through to Staines. The front four carriages went forward to Virginia Water, the rear four coaches in which I travelled ran through to Datchet and Windsor, formerly known as Windsor & Eton Riverside station. On the journey home I would continue to read my morning paper, *The Guardian*. Most commuters would be reading one of the two London evening papers.

I had only been working a few days at Hardcastle's when a serious calamity befell the city. The Grocers' Livery Hall caught fire in the afternoon. Princes Street and Gresham Street were strewn with firemen's hoses. It was a sad loss as their ancient Hall had had a particularly fine Victorian makeover. They lost all their muniments which, of course, were irreplaceable.

It was during this time at Hardcastle's that the Profumo affair broke upon the country. John Profumo, the then Secretary of State for War, had a scandalous affair with an attractive young lady called Christine Keeler. Commuters would read in their newspapers the latest revelations, morning after morning, before the other news and sports stories. I kept every *Guardian* press cutting carefully but in clearing up twenty years later, I threw them away. Now I wish that I had made a proper dossier of the cuttings, as I am sure that it would have been eagerly sought after by some collector.

In Stoke Newington in North London there were two elderly gentlemen, H. & H. Bristow, who traded as local furniture removers. They had quickly established the business during the Second World War, taking advantage of people needing to move during the bombing of London. Their removal business boomed and the company was split into two when they acquired a second depot for the removal vans and extra offices. For us at Hardcastle's, it was a chance to earn some Saturday overtime, as the Bristows were too busy to have us around during the working week. The removal men would be washing down the vans or tinkering with their motors if they too were prepared to work overtime on Saturday afternoon. We would visit one depot once a year on a day that suited one H. Bristow and then go to his brother's depot on another Saturday. It was a typical happily run family firm. When it was decided which days we would visit it behoved us to telephone one of the Mr Bristows. He had very ill-fitting dentures and everyone waited to see how I restrained my giggle when he answered their telephone number "CLIsschold double shix double shix". Each year this would become the amusement of the month in our dull clerks' office.

I cannot remember when I first sat the Institute of Chartered Accountants intermediate exam. It was certainly while I was at Hardcastle's, but I failed at my first attempt. I re-sat the exams in 1966 but got a poor pass numbered 1154 on the list of successful candidates. It was clear that I needed wider accounting experience if I was to get through the finals, so I approached a firm of accountancy personnel agents for some interviews. They found me two companies: one offered £600 a year and the other, which specialised in underwriting, offered £750. I first went for an interview at one in Blomfield Street where a very large office had been divided into several small ones by means of an expanse of beautiful shoulder-height mahogany partitioning arching over every doorway.

I was more comfortable with the interview at a firm called Longcrofts' in nearby New Broad Street. At the interview I stipulated that if my work was satisfactory, my £600 a year salary should be augmented to £625 in three months' time. My proposal was accepted.

I then saw Mr John to tell him I felt that I had learned all I could at Hardcastle's and that I needed wider experience if I was to become a chartered accountant. He seemed sorry but I reminded him that I had failed the intermediate exam at my first sitting. We agreed that I should work on until he could find a replacement and he soon recruited a fair-headed young man who enjoyed cross-country running. Once I had left the company I never saw any of the staff again, even on the City streets.

So it was that in September 1966 I moved my place of work the short distance from Hardcastle's offices at South Place to Longcrofts' in New Broad Street. Reginald Stoddard Longcroft, who with his sons also owned Trinidad Canadian Oil Ltd, headed the company. The family had created Longcrofts' by merging a number of other London firms. They took the best audits for themselves and their staff, while the personal tax, plus smaller audits, were assigned to the other partners. I was first attached to Mr Gerald Bunker, who was in dire need of staff to clear a great backlog of audits. He scarcely had the office space to accommodate the necessary filing as well as all his clerks. His own secretary had her desk in one corner of his room and usually had to stop typing on her clattering typewriter whenever a client visited him. If Mr Bunker's discussions were yet further prolonged more and more of the staff became idle because they thought that files they sought might be in Mr Bunker's occupied room. Needless to say many files got forgotten in this way and were lost for several days.

His general staff room was no larger than that of the clerks' at Hardcastle's. But there were now eight of us, plus a large Rank

Xerox photocopier, which all of the firm's clerks and secretaries had to share. Their frequent visits to the copier caused yet more interruptions to the clerical work. There was another one, in the rooms of the oil company, which we were not allowed to use. On the few occasions when ours broke down, we crossed the road to the offices of Roney & Co., an obliging firm of solicitors, to use their machine.

A two-partner accountancy practice had offices upstairs. In those days, under the Institute's regulations, chartered accountants in practice were not allowed to have more than about four clerks articled to each of them. Accordingly I had been attached to Mr Heller, the younger partner in the upstairs firm which, until it had merged with Longcrofts, had been run by a whiskered Dickensian character named Mr Holt. They and their staff upstairs were scarcely ever seen by the rest of us.

Having met Mr Heller, and shaken hands with him on my first day with the firm, he didn't speak to me for months. Even now I am puzzled as to why the Institute insisted on a nominated principal being allotted to each clerk. He never reviewed my work or gave me any advice.

There had been very little chatter in the clerks' room at Hardcastle's, but here at Longcrofts there was a continuous flow from nearly everyone. Undoubtedly there were too many 20-year-olds in one small room. One day, someone announced that if you picked out the letters on a telephone dial and dialled OBSCENITY you would be answered by the toll-keeper of Clifton Suspension Bridge. For the rest of the morning we all took it in turns on our telephones to see if it was true. With kids in other offices all across England doing this, the toll-keeper must have been at his wits' end in answering "Clifton Suspension Bridge" only to hear "Sorry, wrong number!" This gave me an idea to see how many of the trunk calls I might dial to friends and relations could be memorised easily by such mnemonics. I found, for example, that my first cousin in Grace Darling's former cottage at Bamburgh could easily be reached by dialling ODAL-SKODAL.

When the General Post Office changed the subscriber trunk dialling prefix from 0 to 01 one just needed to remember to insert the new 1 in order to carry on as before. In many cases the mnemonic has to be prefixed by 01.

Mr Bunker's tranche of clients included two Greek gentlemen who I believe were brothers. They owned two rather seedy restaurants in Hanway Street close to Tottenham Court Road underground station. Hanway Street was part of an older road system most of which had long been cleared away for redevelopment of Oxford Street and as we revelled the 'back alley' atmosphere was soon forgotten. I had worked on the books of the two brothers and decided to hold my 21st birthday party there. It was the custom in those days to 'come of age' at 21 rather than 18. I had saved up to entertain my colleagues, though this was largely unnecessary as Mr Bunker provided a respectable sum of money towards the event. The basement of one restaurant was set out for the party.

One colleague had brought a friend from another firm and we noted that by the end of the evening the latter had spent the entire time very deep in conversation with Mr Bunker's secretary. It was clearly love at first sight and within a year they were married.

One of Mr Holt and Mr Heller's staff was a very competent young lady accountant, Linda Gracie. She was already chartered and was brilliant at tax. The only other women were the secretaries and the Comptometer operators. In those days Comptometer operators were always kept happy because with their machines they could add up a column of 52 figures in just a few seconds. However, we men had to carry their very heavy confounded machines for them whenever they had to work at our clients'.

At Hardcastle's, I do not think that any of the clerks ever dated the secretaries. The Palmers usually employed older ladies and we did not discuss our private lives.

Having settled in at Longcrofts I was first allotted the task of closing down a range of dormant companies. Two of us were employed on the enterprise but after the first five companies the job had become most soul-destroying. We worked on over forty defunct businesses. It was a new experience and happily it was the last time that I undertook such a job. Like the 'old pub jobs', I was learning what types of client I did not want to undertake if ever I went into practice. I was beginning to feel that Mr Bunker had a 'rum lot' of clients from which he could not extricate himself. I was pleased never to have to do such a task again.

After a few days in Mr Bunker's department his manager, Mr Arthur Hooper, told me that I was to go down to Hampshire, where I was to work on the books of one of Mr Bunker's elderly relatives. Our office had been unable to find any files for her previous year's accounts and there was no trial balance from which I could work or any analysis of prior year debtors and creditors. The lady's personal chauffeur met me at the railway station and he was to take me back to the return train to Waterloo that evening. The lady neither greeted me nor came to see what I was doing and I didn't know what I was supposed to be doing. I was never to meet our client. I was taken into an office, where a bookkeeper sat and where I worked for the rest of the morning. Nobody told me what her business was and I was too reserved to ask. I managed to analyse the bankings and all of the cheques drawn. However, when I needed the records of the petty cash spent the bookkeeper had already left so I did the best I could.

When back in London the next day, I told Mr Bunker that I could only do what was possible. It transpired that the lady had complained to Mr Bunker that I had not left her bookkeeper a list of questions and that she felt that my visit was a waste of time. I agreed with him and said I was very uncomfortable about not having been briefed on her type of business or the object of my visit and my not having had any trial balance and working papers from the close of the previous year.

I suspected that they had been fobbing her off with 'waiting for new staff' until I had arrived. None of us clerks ever heard of the job again, much to our relief. She probably found a local firm to see to her accounts, which was what she should have done in the first place.

Unfortunately, this was typical of some of the jobs that had been allocated to Mr Bunker. Nowadays I feel that he must have despaired at the situation but he was locked into the partnership. He had many disordered tasks which could not have been profitable either to him or to the firm.

I had also begun to recognise the problems which result from leaving prior papers in such an untidy state. When at Hardcastle's we formally closed off an account's year with a bank reconciliation, closing lists of debtors and creditors and trial balances. This was *de rigueur* at Hardcastle's but was not a standard procedure at Longcrofts' or at the firms from which the papers had previously come. I'm sure that I was wise not to have remained to qualify at Hardcastle's, as Jeffrey Tye had done. In no way would Mr John Palmer have sent me out without prior guidance for the year to be tackled.

With hindsight Mr John would certainly have inculcated us clerks with a good practical audit system, if Hardcastle's had had better accounting jobs to work on at the time. Some time after I had left Hardcastle's, Mr John Palmer had selected new partners who gave the firm higher prestige. He headed it from new offices, no great distance from his home in Cuffley. I am not sure when his father, Mr Arthur, retired but I am sure he would have continued enjoying his golf. Longcrofts had several potentially good audits. Unfortunately there was no uniform audit system set up across the firm so we articled clerks could not follow on with each client year upon year. We would read the Institute's magazine articles about new techniques in auditing, but they all seemed rather mysterious to us.

It was a shame that in those days it was all too easy to get a practising certificate from the Institute of Chartered Accountants. There was a rule that you had to ask for one if you earned even one small private fee. The Institute was keen to collect a charge and annual renewal subscription without regard to the individual's efficacy.

I received my certificate in 1971 and it was to be 25 years before anyone at the Institute ever came to check on my quality control. Around the country there must have been many chartered accountants who had worked for several years without regard to setting their own standards for clients. Even then I was only marked down on my failing to keep photocopies of client tax returns on file. I appealed and was able to satisfy them that I had an analysis of every figure in the tax return in my papers and therefore did not need to make a copy of a tax return where several of the pages had no entries put in each tax return which usually took up only a third of a page instead of the sixteen pages which the Institute wanted to see. This meant that the Inspector only required the total dividend figure in the tax return whereas a good accountant would have a full analysis of the client's dividends in order to check whether any were missed in the following year's tax return details. It amazed me that the Institute wanted to see sixteen pages of photocopying of the return without the analysis that I would keep with my short summary. The Institute had no idea how to save paper in order to highlight information. Nevertheless, I never had an enquiry from the Revenue about, for example, a declared summary dividend figure, in over 40 years in practice.

This extended summary of my clients' tax returns, listed each Gift Aid, building society interest, bank interest, employment, etc. I was thus able to watch out for all of the important components in the next year. It was not something of which I was proud. To me, it was common sense to work in this way. The Institute's Quality Controller upheld my appeal. He agreed that my system was actually better than photocopying the Inland Revenue's official form, which only gave summary totals. I had won my point and continued with my own system. That was to be the only visit from the Institute's standards officer in all my forty-four years as an accountant 'in practice'.

Longcrofts' had taken over a firm of accountants and financial advisers called Buxton, Beresford & Co. for whom Mr Bunker was required to bring the clients' accounts up to date with no previous working papers provided. As regards clients taken over from other firms, Arthur Hooper handed me the previous year's papers.

It was clear that Buxton, Beresford & Co. had never shown their clients how to prepare or summarise their accounts for an audit properly. There was no equivalent of the clerk who at J. Carroll & Sons would turn the papers into a takings book and neatly sequence the bank statements for us. Matters seemed worse when I told Arthur I could not find the last trial balance. He told me that Buxton, Beresford & Co. did not usually prepare one and that I would have to work from the previous balance sheet of which we had no analysis, nor could I find any analyses for debtors and creditors or a list of fixed assets. It took a lot of work to get any papers together to start the new year's audit and accounts. I commented to Arthur that the firm had surely risked a reprimand from Companies House and Arthur shared my concern, agreeing with my 'rum lot' comment. I told Mr. Bunker that the sleuthing around was taking as much time as progressing the figures. He had heard all this before and had to alert the clients to being charged a two-year fee.

Hardcastle's had a system of differing ticks which we used on the client's books and our working papers, indicating when a particular task had been completed such as adding up, cross-casting and bringing totals forward. I continued with this simple tick system throughout my self-employment career. I asked Arthur what system of ticks was used at Longcrofts. He told me there was no such system. Suddenly I was proud of having been so well disciplined in good standards at Hardcastle's. There was no way that Buxton, Beresford & Co. could ever have presented a working papers schedule to an enquiring Tax Inspector. My mind boggled as to how on earth they practised as Chartered Accountants. They were obviously a very poor advocate of the Institute's aspirations but in my experience the Institute had not been imposing standards on member firms. I was certainly learning how not to run a firm of Chartered Accountants in the

1960s. I vowed that if I ever took on private clients the first thing to do was to give them a list of what was needed each year. I would expect simple totals for each heading of expenses, lists of dividends and of interest received.

In this way Arthur and I gradually established a neat system for the clients allocated to me as we brought the accounts up to date. I began to find that I was taking on more varied tasks and was being sent out to work at other clients' premises as part of an audit.

This was when I discovered precisely what the office's two Comptometer operator girls did. The heavy machines were carried in special cases and had a number of rows of keys with numbers on them. The girls would punch the keys with their fingers, several at a time, and thereby add up long columns or whole pages of figures very quickly. They could check column totals and cross-casts and so on. There were also ways to get the machines to multiply and divide entirely mechanically.

The operators' abilities were impressive. Like the audit staff on bigger jobs, they might be expected to stay overnight at a hotel. When they were in the office these girls could be a nuisance if left idle and bored. When necessary they were expected to operate the telephone switchboard, pulling corded plugs in and out of the ancient switchboard terminals. At other times they would come into our eight-staff office and interrupt us with their chat. They were always very over-perfumed.

It was obvious who had dated them the previous evening and soon we all learnt about it. On a daily basis we were guilty of idle chatter and no one seemed to be able to deal with telephone calls quietly. With all of the interruptions we became used to Mr Bunker's exasperated flying visits when he found that jobs were not being finished speedily.

In Hardcastle's clerks' office, none of us had ever spoken about girlfriends. Maybe no one had one. But now, in Mr Bunker's clerks' office, the silence was frequently interrupted with the plans and reports of their dates disturbing everyone else's concentration. Each of us would let our minds wander.

Longcrofts senior clerk was a very handsome, well-built man with black hair and deep-set brown eyes. He had broken the hearts of both of our Comptometer operators but was very discreet about it. They would comfort each other in office hours. Whenever they were not sent out to a client to check page upon page of additions in ledgers, they sat in the clerks' office. The handsome clerk soon advanced to become a partner in the firm.

Quite rightly the Comptometer operators refused to trudge to and from the railway stations with their heavy machines. The cost of their taxis was phenomenal. This spelled the demise of the Comptometer operators. It was not until 1971 that desk calculators began to be introduced into accountants' offices and the fate of Comptometer operators was forever sealed, as we were able to work quickly and efficiently on the schedules of figures ourselves.

One day a quiet young man in Mr Bunker's clerks' office announced that he was to be married in a month's time. He would need three weeks off for his honeymoon, taking two weeks' paid leave and one unpaid. We had a whip-round in the office and off he went for the great event. Only two weeks later he reappeared. We soon learnt the sorry story that on their wedding night his bride had refused to sleep with him. She had screamed and run out of the hotel. The poor man returned to the office terribly depressed and left the firm later that year. At least he had qualified as a chartered accountant with Longcrofts'.

The shock of the incident put an end to idle gossip about girlfriends for several weeks. I think that we all concentrated on our work more sedulously than ever before.

After six months at Longcrofts' I went to see James Longcroft's brother, the man who had first interviewed me. I asked whether I could have the salary rise from £600 p.a. to £625 p.a., which had been agreed if my first six months' work were satisfactory. I pointed out that I had largely cleared up the Buxton, Beresford shambles. He agreed without hesitation and asked me to fetch the wages clerk, who was a gruff old man with an office to himself. His walls were decorated with Inland Revenue announcements and leaflets. A brief glance at these revealed that they mostly dealt with changes to Double Tax Treaties with other countries, certainly irrelevant to the greater part of Longcrofts' client portfolio.

Longcrofts' founder, the elderly Reginald Stoddart Longcroft, was a man who for reasons not known to us hated Germans. One day he needed a lift in Gerald Bunker's car. Suddenly Gerald realised that he had a very tricky situation in carrying such a man in his BMW car. Mr Longcroft congratulated him on his choice of such a smooth-running, comfortable vehicle, and asked Gerald what the initials 'BMW' stood for. He hesitated before replying 'British Motor Works'. Back in the office he related the incident to all of us who were present. He added that for a moment he feared that Reginald might have demanded to get out of the car and insist on taking a taxi for the rest of the journey.

This tale amused the entire office throughout the following week.

Later I felt confident enough to go to Mr Bunker to ask if I could be given tax work to help me with my studies. He was in a good mood and told me that his partner Mr Cunningham was to run a tax seminar later in the month. All we clerks would be expected to attend. For this Longcrofts hired the Little Ship Club on the Thames waterfront, next to Southwark Bridge. The lecture was to be about the new Corporation Tax, which had just been introduced. Every technical member of staff was required to attend. Sensibly the seating at the club had been arranged with our backs to the view of the river. Some caterers wheeled in trolleys laden with tea, coffee, biscuits and crockery on cue for the mid-morning break. They took it all away before Mr Cunningham's second lecture but a half-hour later they started to bring in everything for lunch. I was seated near to the tables. Unfortunately the clatter of the best china and metal cutlery made it impossible for most of us to hear Mr. Cunningham's lecture properly. He had a quiet voice and the firm had not opted to pay extra for a public address system. Wisely he delayed the start of his third lecture until the caterers had cleared up the lunch, but by then he had lost what voice he did have.

A different partner in the firm, Mr James Calver-Jones, saw the problem and took the stand from the voiceless Mr Cunningham. He gave an impromptu summary of recent changes to the income and corporation tax systems. Still his voice was also rather weak and some members of the audience became restless in their squeaky chairs. Needless to say the day was a complete disaster and there was a general consensus that nobody had learnt as much as had been hoped unless they were in the front row away from the clattering of crockery. Perhaps, if Mr Cunningham had prepared a printed synopsis of his lecture the day might not have been such a disappointment. All that we could do was to sit and listen.

The main lesson learnt that day was the preparation of a lecture and how important it was that PA systems, clattering cutlery and crockery should be taken into account!

My lack of experience in Income Tax was continuing to retard my progress towards exams so I went to the office upstairs to talk to Mr Heller, to whom I was articled. He did not recognise me and I had to remind him that we had not spoken since we had signed my Articles of Clerkship fifteen months earlier. I told him that I would be taking my finals in the next year and asked if I could transfer to work under Mr Calver-Jones to learn more about personal tax. He said that he needed time to discuss it with the other partners.

I asked Mr Heller whether he had been writing the reports to the Institute about my progress. He told me that he had signed the reports but that Mr Bunker had written them. This distance between an articled clerk and his principal clarifies how outdated the Institute's Articles' requirement had already become. My appeal for the transfer was seen as a problem. Mr Bunker felt that he still needed me on his non-tax work. So then I took my request for tax experience to Mr Longcroft and reminded him of our first meeting. I told him that I had left my previous firm because I was lacking experience in taxation and was still lacking it now. Shortly afterwards Mr Longcroft set in motion arrangements for me to transfer six weeks later to Mr Calver-Jones. This left Mr Bunker having to find a new clerk to do my work, which of course led to clients being annoyed that they got a different clerk every year or so instead of someone who had working experience in their business. However, from the firm's point of view clients are only stepping stones in a clerk's progress to accountancy qualifications.

Mr Calver-Jones was glad to take me into his group of clerks as he had lately had to ask an agency to find him someone for tax work. One downside for me was that an incomplete records job was coming in shortly and he wanted me to do it, he pleading with me to do just this one awkward task. In the meantime I started learning personal tax. I was content. Mr Calver-Jones' standards and his working papers were far better than Mr Bunker's. I found that it was easy to do the same schedules as the previous year, even the tax computation. He took a healthy interest in what his staff could do and checked everything. He taught me a lot.

When the incomplete records job arrived, a mass of papers in a large box, it transpired that it was from his neighbour, a farmer deep in the country. The farmer had no system of recording receipts and invoices or any system based on his bank statements. I told Mr Calver-Jones that I had been unable to find any copies of invoices issued by the farmer and could he please fetch them. A few days later he told me that there were no copy invoices. Apparently the farm was run largely on cash and barter. This was just the sort of business that would not be able to cope with the introduction of Value Added Tax five years later. I think that Mr Calver-Jones was very upset with himself for having agreed to take on this client and I believe he took the job home and did it himself. Certainly none of us ever again saw the job in the office.

Another newly introduced tax was Selective Employment Tax. This was very ill conceived by a government in panic mode and it did not last for many months. During that time employers and firms of accountancy had spent a fortune training their staff to deal with it. Mr Calver-Jones was just about to give his entire department a long lecture about it when the government announced it was abolishing the tax! Today it is but a distant memory of an ill-advised government scheme. At Longcrofts' we had had to add an extra sixpence per hour to our individual fee-charging rates. To give Longcrofts' credit, they did cancel the sixpence charge when the tax was abolished, yet other firms treated it as a permanent rise in their fees.

In Mr Calver-Jones' clerks' office there were just two ladies. One was an elderly Serbo-Croat with a loud telephone voice, while the other was his secretary. The clattering of her electric typewriter would have been a distraction to Mr Calver-Jones' numerous visiting clients, so she was installed in his clerk's office.

In Mr Calver-Jones' group we seemed to be much happier and better focussed on our work than were Mr Bunker's clerks down the corridor. I was learning quickly and really enjoying the income and the newly introduced capital gains tax work.

The time of my final exams was approaching so I was delighted when Mr. Calver-Jones asked me if I would like the firm to pay for me to go on a revision course for a few weeks. It was run by H. Foulkes Lynch & Co. Ltd, and was time really well spent.

A few weeks earlier Mr Calver-Jones had asked me if I would accept as a personal client one of his own client's bookkeepers as our firm's fees could not be justified on so small a task. It transpired that she was the client's general factotum who wanted help claiming relief for mortgage interest against her income tax under the rules then in force.

I was very pleased that a partner had selected me from his staff to help this young lady on my own terms. Longcrofts' company employees were not allowed to take on private clients so the offer came as a great surprise to me. While it would impinge on my time for studies I was indeed excited at the prospect. I went to meet her that evening and clearly remember both the place and date; it was 13th January 1969 at 24 Tottenham Street.

During my earliest years in the Institute of Chartered Accountants we members were not allowed to advertise our services beyond putting a plaque at the office door. This did not trouble me as I was still employed by a City firm. So I took on some more private clients rather lightheartedly. Until 1971 I volunteered as a scoutmaster with a troop of boys at Ruislip on the edge of northwest London. Through this occupation I was introduced to six new clients, the first of whom was an enterprising young car mechanic at Harefield. As the year progressed I accepted more requests to work privately. All were short-term, one or two-year jobs, except the car mechanic. From the outset he was keen to have his books and accounts done correctly by a chartered accountant. His father was the manager of a sewage pumping station with a cottage and garage nearby. The mechanic had quickly gained a good reputation for his vehicle repairs and after enlarging the garage to become a workshop, he was lucky to attract as customers some of the employees of the local Uxbridge Council. This was his insurance against being shut down by the Council for any technical reason about trading illicitly on the Council's private lane to the sewerage works. I have never known anyone else treble the size of his premises without having to make umpteen planning applications! He also hired a council bulldozer on a barter arrangement to create a parking area further down the lane near the pumping station for customers' cars and wrecks. His prowess as a mechanic was beyond that of most motor engineers and he always burnished his customers' cars beautifully before they collected them.

I applied all I that I had learned at Hardcastle's on the mechanic's accounts. The first set covered an entire year to May and had rather a large sum for capital introduced into the business. The Inland Revenue inspector decided he could not have derived it from savings and raised an enquiry. My client admitted that he had bought his private car, a spectacular old Aston Martin DB5, for £1,150 of undeclared earnings and not savings.

The inspector in the local Uxbridge tax office was lenient and my client had already learned his lesson: so had I.

Despite the good training that I had had at Hardcastle's I would never prepare another sole trader or sole practitioner balance sheet unless it was really necessary. I continued to do the car mechanic's accounts and taxes with never another enquiry from the tax office or a VAT inspection. We only parted company after 27 years because I had become too expensive for his business. Over those years he had also nursed along his Aston Martin DB5 and even sent it for classic car treatment. I hope he still has it.

My fourth client was the bookkeeper at Hallett, Fox & White. We had kept in contact from my days at Hardcastle's, their auditors.

My first big chance in gaining clients came in the autumn of 1970. For some years I had had an interest in the silent cinema and was subscribing to a new and well-written magazine named *The Silent Picture*. I enquired about a particular film called *The Accidental Champion*' at the British Film Institute in Dean Street, London and I was referred to the editor of the cinema magazine, Anthony Slide, who was expected to visit later that evening. I asked him if he was getting tax loss relief for his acclaimed magazine. A month later he got in touch with me and became my eighth client. As soon as his tax refund reached him he introduced me to a friend who was a pianist at the National Film Theatre. He in turn then introduced me to yet another pianist who had recently graduated from London's Trinity College of Music and who, along with three girlfriends was embarking on a self-employed career and who were in need of an accountant who understood musicians. They all became my clients.

The Silent Picture served its purpose in that my client procured a top job at the American Film Institute so he closed down its London operation and I procured his final British tax loss repayment for him after which he emigrated to California. Amazingly, this magazine, which had only run for four years, is still very highly spoken of in vintage film circles.

By 1983 I had amassed as many clients as I could handle, with musicians being by far the greatest proportion. Had I not set up arrangements for the overflow of clients to another firm, I would have found myself called upon to handle about 1,300 self-employed persons in professions and vocations. Most of my clientele were musicians and singers, all of whom had been trained to work under the baton of a conductor and therefore knew the consequences of not following the professional advice that I was giving them. Sometimes these people working in music introduced relatives who might be editors, designers, writers, etc., while perhaps half a dozen of my clients came through my interest in American and Western Europe vintage silent film.

I was often invited to their concerts which would conclude with a glass of wine in the Green Room. More often than not I would then be introduced to yet another lately qualified musician who was seeking an accountant. In such a case I would suggest that they get in touch with me on another day. In that way I would be able to assure myself that the person who had recommended me was already a satisfactory client. Otherwise I would politely say that my books were full for the present.

By this method I reckon that I avoided nearly every person who might have proved difficult. A long personal discussion on the telephone was all I needed to identify sincere and responsible potential clients.

During my time at Hardcastle's I had learnt the importance of attention to detail, something which actually came easily to me. At Longcrofts, I had then learned how crucial it is to direct clients to present their data clearly to their tax accountants. Mr Calver-Jones, with his zeal for the subject, had given me a thorough grounding in personal taxation. I was able to apply all those well-learned skills to help me to establish my own business.

I resolved to ask that each of my music clients work through a list of over one hundred headings of expenses which were likely to apply to them. I adapted the list for each new person and then asked them to calculate a total figure for each of the appropriate headings. I also asked them for a total of fees received plus expenses reimbursed from each engagement as well as for any P60 or PAYE forms and for all vouchers associated with foreign tax, but no other business vouchers unless and until requested. I urged everyone to keep an annual folder of all vouchers which I had not sought and to summarise those vouchers carefully, ready for comparison with figures in the accounts I prepared in case an inspector raised an enquiry.

Deciding on the date of commencement of business was in the eyes of tax inspectors a 'matter of fact'. All of our detailed groundwork helped me to present clearly correct figures and claims to the Inland Revenue. Many of my clients would find themselves following this rubric for over thirty years. I would invariably head my annual fee-note '30th' annual fee-note or '35th' annual fee-note as appropriate, briefly stunning the client that he had been in business and under my care for so long.

If a client did not need to claim a cost under one of the headings I would nonetheless type the heading in the accounts, specifically marked £0, so that the tax inspector would be aware that we were not claiming for every conceivable heading, only for the relevant ones. This was good 'inspector psychology' to indicate that we knew the rules that he wanted us to follow. In consequence I never had an enquiry on some clients' accounts in forty years. I would recommend this ploy to any accountant working with such people as musicians and singers. A few clients questioned why there were such blank entries in their accounts and I happily told them of this 'psychology' ploy, which greatly comforted them.

In due course I sat the Institute's finals examination. Of course I was very disappointed when I failed the paper on corporation tax, my weakest subject. It meant that I would have to re-sit the exams six months later. Mr. Calver-Jones found that he would no longer be able to afford me on my substantial salary and he had to seek a replacement who would take a lower wage. He gently suggested that I should aim to join a larger firm for more corporation tax experience.

It was fortunate that I already knew someone who worked at the company of accountants Touche Ross (then known as Touche Ross Bailey & Smart). He suggested that I telephone for an interview.

Their recruitment officer told me that there was a post in

the corporation tax department that handled partnership tax so I would not be involved solely in corporation tax. I said that I would welcome partnership tax experience but did not wish to handle any more individual tax clients. This suited Touche Ross well so we agreed on a salary of £2,800 p.a. to rise to £3,200 p.a. when I passed the finals examination. They would also pay for me to go on a further revision course before the examinations. Happily this time I passed.

One of the young managers at Touche Ross for whom I was to work was Tom Lane. He had joined at around the same time as me, having worked as an inspector in a district tax office. He had become disillusioned with the Inland Revenue and the quality of the staff there. Tom was a remarkably intelligent young man: decisive, knowledgeable and very easy to work with. He never got frustrated or short-tempered and explained issues clearly. I could see he was a significant loss to the Inland Revenue.

I was planning to have a crack at the Associate examination for the Institute of Taxation. I told Tom, he took a look at the syllabus for this Institute's Fellowship exam and decided he would sit for that. In May 1969 we both sat and passed these exams. Unfortunately, he soon became disillusioned with Touche Ross & Co. and left the company. I never heard from him again. However, I found out that he had set up his own practice and I hope surrounded himself with the clients whom he deserved and who respected him. I now know that he emigrated to Australia, where he has run his own sizeable taxation firm successfully. I was glad that Tom had resigned from working under the appallingly arrogant partner Maurice Thomsett, and obviously fared far better in Australia.

In those days Touche Ross occupied a number of offices on various levels in the southeast quadrant of Finsbury Circus, fronting London Wall to the south and Blomfield Street to the east. The notepaper proclaimed the firm as Touche, Ross & Co. and on the next line, Touche Ross, Bailey & Smarts. This presumably reflected a merger earlier in the 1960s. There was also, somewhere along our upstairs corridor, an independent company called Touche Remnant.

One morning after I had walked into the office from Cannon Street Station and begun working at my desk, a colleague named Lester Child went straight to his desk and at once rang the Metropolitan police to report that he had just observed his sports car, stolen from him several months earlier, parked in Finsbury Circus close to the office building. It was a car he had cherished but it had a minor defect which he recognised when he had paused to admire it. Although it had a changed number plate, Lester still had a document bearing the chassis number equally close to his heart in his wallet. He told us that the police wished him to go to the vehicle and wait for an officer to arrive. The police duly checked the vehicle and confirmed the chassis number. Lester was asked to return to the car after an hour, while waiting for the second hour on the parking meter to begin. In the meantime police presumably carried out checks back to the original number plate and then the present owner. On returning to his car, this man was asked by the officer how he had come by the car and made to hand over the keys. The police officer then drove it away and some days later the stolen car, non the worse for wear, was formally reunited with a very contented Lester Child, who obviously gained some 'brownie points' from his insurance company!

Occasionally one had to set off on a hike along the other floors of the building. We would need to find our typing pool (as nobody typed their own letters in those days) or the personal tax department, or to search for the partners' rooms in some distant corner of the building. At least the lifts never seemed to be out of action. It was in fact a very pleasant place for us all.

One day I paused at the lift near the Administration Department and noticed a huge pile of partly opened packs of company notepaper. As usual it named every single partner as required by the Partnership Act of the day. It was beautifully thermographed, an impressive presentation that not many firms bespeak these days. I then realised that Touche had been spelt

Touch throughout the vast consignment and that it was awaiting collection for pulping. It was an extremely expensive mistake on someone's part.

After being with Touche Ross for a few weeks, I had a call from Jim Calver-Jones at Longcrofts'. He had made each of us retain a copy of the letters that we wrote in a blue file. He wondered if I still had mine and I told him that I had. It was obvious that I should not have kept the file and I took it back. In doing so I took the opportunity to discuss with him my second personal client, the mechanic who had bought a second-hand Aston Martin DB5, and I formally thanked him for the personal tax training which was obviously standing me in good stead for the future. I did not know at the time that his share of clients was not a very profitable enterprise, given the high rent paid by Longcroft's on their rather fine suite of offices in New Broad Street, and I think this must have distressed him.

At Touche Ross I was allocated a desk in the Corporation Tax clerks' room. It was next to the office of Mr Douglas Morpeth, one of the most senior partners in the firm. He was a charming man with a genuine smile and a memorable full head of silver hair. Oddly he always appeared to have tinted his eyebrows jet black. I can never recall his ever being frustrated or angry.

Like John Palmer of Hardcastle's, Mr Morpeth was also an officer at the Honourable Artillery Company in City Road. Here he went to great efforts to amalgamate the Association of Certified Accountants with the Institute of Chartered Accountants in England and Wales. Apparently the Certified Accountants had merged much earlier with another body where exams had been less demanding on its students and the Chartered members considered them to have qualified far too easily. Accordingly he could not generate enough support for the merger, and as the members had voted against the proposal he had to cease negotiation. He was later knighted. We were very pleased for him.

My first assignment at Touche Ross was the corporation tax of Constellation Investments Ltd. Previously I had been impressed that Mr Calver-Jones had a major television personality's tax account to handle, but Constellation had a veritable cast list of famous people many of whom are well known even today, 47 years later.

The scheme that Touche Ross had arranged for Constellation meant that its clients would let the company receive all their future earnings. In return, they were granted debentures which were quoted on the London Stock Exchange at a nominal sum. In payment the company retained a commission on the personalities' entire earnings. It would release to their clients an appropriate number of their debentures, which could then be sold on the Stock Exchange when they chose to do so. The corporation tax paid by the company, plus the capital gains tax paid by the celebrities, was always less than the very high rates of income tax that the celebrity would have had to pay were they not debenture holders. When I arrived on the scene several of these stars had already earned the release of all their debentures and sold them on the Stock Market for capital gains which after tax left them with more net income than if they simply suffered income tax and surtax on fees earned. The entire scheme was quashed by Section 31 of the Finance Act 1969. It was a 'tax loophole' which the government had never previously sought to close. I never understood why something so simple had not been considered years before the tax was introduced on capital gains. My first main job at Touche Ross was to clear up the tax ramifications of this defunct scheme, which had been marvellous while it had been legitimate. It had been a wonderful four-year tax holiday for several famous names in British entertainment. I very much pitied the people in Constellation when it befell me to help wind up the Constellation scheme in the wake of that new legislation.

On reflection I could not have joined Touche Ross & Co. at a more propitious time. Within months of joining the firm I passed the final exam to become a chartered accountant in May 1969. As previously arranged my salary was raised to the £3,200 discussed earlier. Thereafter I received a pay rise every six months.

A week after I had qualified, I received a letter of congratulation from Mr Arthur Palmer at Hardcastle's. To be truthful, I had given Hardcastle's very little thought since my leaving them three and half years earlier. Indeed they were a happy little firm and had taught me to add 52-figure columns quickly, trial balance and simple accounting with balance sheets, but after two years I had no idea of simple taxation even for sole traders. At Longcrofts', Jim Calver-Jones had proved that I had a penchant for personal income tax, but the firm had no audit manual and was disgraced when his auditing technique failed to find that a member of the accountancy team in the oil distribution company near Bedford had been teeming and lading cheques received. I had learned from the revelations the sorts of things to which auditors need to be alert. At no stage in my time at Hardcastle's had I helped in any bankruptcy or liquidation, yet there were questions on these situations in the Institute of Chartered Accountants' examinations, albeit rather superficial ones. There were no questions set on accounts for underwriters and I could have gone 'that way' if I had joined a firm desperately offering an extra 25% salary above that offered by Longcrofts. I suppose I should have ignored Mr Arthur's letter but I felt strongly about my lack of experience in taxation and wrote back to him outlining the shortcomings in his approach to training an articled clerk and why I had left. It must have upset him but it may have been the fillip which the firm needed, for Mr John soon led the firm forward, taking on good work and extra partners to build it up to the HB Accountants that it is today in Hertfordshire.

Touche Ross had an impressive number of City stockbrokers as clients. The issue at the time was whether the brokers should incorporate as Limited Companies following a relaxation in rules by the Stock Exchange Council or carry on as partnerships. In those days there was a particular scheme. Each time a partner was appointed or resigned, all the partners decided whether to elect on the old business continuing into the new partnership. We could see how the Revenue might legislate to defeat the scheme but all they did was to make the tax slightly less avoidable. It was not until the advent of self-assessment in 1997 that they were to minimalise the extensive benefits which partnerships had enjoyed for decades. The Touche Ross partner for whom I worked was Derek Chapman. He was a very quiet and gifted man and I really enjoyed working with him. I would assemble the figures and summarise my calculations and he would then visit the particular stockbroking partnership to discuss them and the options. Derek may have brought one or two more stockbrokers to Touche Ross for a view as to whether they should forgo their partnership tax advantages by incorporating. I was keenly engaged in calculating alternative strategies for at least three of London's most successful stockbrokers.

The tax partners at Touche Ross gave young Derek Chapman an opportunity to excel when the Council of the London Stock Exchange finally allowed stockbroker partnerships to incorporate. Of course, probably no partnership understood what tax advantages might result from their incorporation. Derek approached the two largest stockbrokers with whom the firm already dealt. He was the ideal man to tackle the task. He spoke clearly and in simple terms and was able to make sure that all the partners understood him.

Derek looked around for someone to work out what in tax terms each election for each partner would mean. I was truly grateful when he selected me to prepare all the calculations for his discussions with one of the partnerships. I was absolutely in my element in this task, fully understanding the value of one election with or instead of another and testing various cessation or continuation dates and other ramifications.

Close on its heels came the second stockbroker firm's figures and criteria, forecasts and preferences. Then the first firm was reworked with actual results and new forecasts, partners, and so on. Then a third and even a fourth firm came to us from other accountants just for this advice. This enjoyable work lasted for almost three years, peppered with more mundane corporation tax work for other clients, none of which was as interesting to me as partnership tax.

I believe that the stockbroker partners looked upon Derek as a magician. I remember thanking him for giving me such a thorough practical experience in partnership tax which I could not have gained in either of my two previous firms nor most likely many other firms in the City of London.

Derek had perceived that I had a clear head for attention to detail. I was taken back to thoughts of my school days when my housemaster declared to me at a half-termly progress review, at the age of 15, "Pedler! You spend far too much time attending to detail." I was certainly confused. How glad I was never to have taken any notice of his rebuke. What a pity for his pupils' sake that he could not recognise and encourage budding talent.

An example of this attention to detail has arisen on the mainline railways in the West Country. The present population of Cullompton and Wellington justifies their stations being reopened. Express trains take 23 minutes to travel from Exeter to Taunton, calling only at Tiverton. There are several times a day when there are more than two express trains in an hour. If stopping trains were introduced to call additionally at these two stations, Cullompton and Wellington, they would take about 38 minutes and an express train would be held up behind stopping trains. This would restrict the frequency of trains or the speed of the express trains, therefore Cullompton and Wellington cannot be reopened. Little problems like this are crystal clear to me but it would take a very gifted man to convey the concept to the townspeople.

From time to time one or two of the firm's own articled clerks would be sent along to the tax department to have hands-on experience of corporation tax work. There was not much we could show them without disrupting our own work schedules. I remember that some weeks after one of these clerks had sat beside me to see how I was working I was sent a follow-up document asking me to say what I though of his work. On the one hand

I could not remember who this clerk was but I just attached a note to the document saying I was not myself a manager and therefore not in a position to comment or criticise the work of another employee. On the other I always found things like this rather distasteful, especially as Touche Ross had its own staff training department and did not need to interrupt its productive staff, who had no idea of the stage reached by the articled clerk in his training.

It was while I was at Touche Ross in 1970 that I was encouraged to have the 'flu jab'. I agreed and there was a mass inoculation on a Friday afternoon in October 1970. The result was that I had a terrible weekend and was scarcely able to get up on the Sunday. I declined it in later years and just as well, for I learned from fellow pupils from my prep school ill in bed with it that in autumn 1957, 92% of the school were laid up with Asian flu and as a result we were immune from all strains of flu ever after. As soon as I had realised this by this wretched experience in 1970 I have always appreciated having suffered the Asian flu at school.

Word spread quickly between stockbroking firms about the quality of Derek's strategic considerations for their tax affairs. It certainly put me in very good stead for considering partnership situations for my clients in future years.

In those days I was appalled by the greed of the partners at Touche Ross & Co. in the matter of billing the clients for our clerical time. Throughout the offices there was a regime which recorded time spent to the nearest half-hour. Each grade of clerk had a charging-out rate that included an allowance for office costs and partner profit. When a periodic bill was due a tax clerk would assemble a summary of monthly time per clerk, manager, Comptometer operator, etc. He would present the tally to the partner, who scrutinised it and returned it to the clerk in order that a fee-note could be prepared and taken to the typing pool up on the top floor, where a typist would prepare the bill which then went to the partner to apply the firm's signature in his own hand.

I noticed that almost every bill was exaggerated to give the partner even more profit allowance. Our charging-out rates were already high without the need for any further increment. Unsurprisingly, this practice often led to clients writing to the partnership in strong terms to challenge the size of the bills.

I was always amazed how several clients of Touche Ross paid such large sums. At Longcrofts' Mr Calver-Jones could give just as good a service at a lesser and very fair fee, even though the City offices of the two firms were only one hundred yards apart.

I recall that the late Cyril Fletcher, the well-known media personality, brought his tax affairs to Touche Ross. Some small firm of accountants had got him into a most frightful mess with the Inland Revenue. Mr Fletcher was pleased with the way Touche Ross cleared everything up for him but then declared that he had to take his affairs elsewhere because of their high level of fees which he could not afford again in this, the autumn of his career. Such was my education in the City. It was not just the ramifications of tax schemes and how to present them on paper but how to account for one's time spent in so doing.

Back at Longcrofts', when Buxton Beresford's accounts were taken on, Gerald Bunker had no difficulty in convincing heavily charged clients that his staff first had a lot to do on the previous year's books. They were already aware that the auditing and filing at that previous firm had been appalling. Gerald's organised and methodical approach ensured that each audit was tidied up and balance sheet schedules were properly prepared.

Down the corridor, Mr Calver-Jones ran excellent tax files but he was poor on his auditing techniques. I remember that a clerk turned up one day from Mr Longcrofts or Mr Gee's department and he started to work on cash book and bank statements for an oil distribution company audit. Within a couple of days he had produced a schedule showing that client moneys had regularly been endorsed into the account of an employee at this oil company. The money only reached the company's bank several weeks later. The employee had had personal cash-flow problems and readily admitted to this 'teeming and lading', but he was able to show that no moneys had been taken on a permanent basis. This had been happening for a long time and I am certain that Mr Calver-Jones would have spotted the problem much earlier had he exercised robust audit procedures. It was in our offices, the event of the year and an important lesson to us all.

The other partners in Longcrofts' took the view that Mr Calver-Jones ought to have spotted this. I presume that he had failed to get the debtor companies to confirm their balances with the oil company at the random mid-year and year-end dates. In hindsight it is easy to suggest that Mr Calver-Jones should have swapped his audits for more personal tax work from his fellow partners.

Touche Ross was keen that there should also be another clerk gaining this experience. So after nearly three years I was transferred to work for another tax partner, Maurice Thomsett. His clients included a car manufacturer in Coventry. Why we had to travel there I have no idea as some of Touche Ross's auditing staff travelled daily in their cars to London. The client had loaned us a car and provided parking at Coventry railway station. I was provided with hotel accommodation in Coventry.

One day I had to meet Maurice Thomsett off a train. Maurice arrived as planned but spent too long chatting about the audit and tax and I could see that I would not be able to fetch the other auditor from the station at the appointed time. I told Mr Thomsett but he would not allow me to go, which I felt was a discourtesy to our colleague. As there was no such thing as a mobile phone in those days, I took it upon myself to drive to the station and fetch our colleague. I returned to find that Mr Thomsett was still in conference but he was extremely annoyed with me. There was no criticism of my work but he declared that he had never been so insulted in all his life. I took him back to the station for his train to London then joined the audit team and we drove to the hotel. The general feeling was that we were all out of our depths with a client of this scale. One day, I was in the room set aside for tax managers at Touche Ross discussing a task with one of the managers Peter Chant, when Mr Thomsett, on returning from seeing a client, suddenly burst in. Rather than ask Peter to come into his room when he would have a free moment, he interrupted our work with a lengthy debriefing of what he had achieved on this other client. He had interrupted all three of the managers in Peter's room and me, without a word of courtesy. His last words were that he was going home as he had nothing else to do! We were all dismayed by his arrogance and resumed the tax work we had been doing. Then Peter and I continued our conversation that had been so rudely interrupted. If Maurice Thomsett had nothing to do for the rest of the afternoon, he could easily have waited until Peter had finished his discussion with me.

While at Touche Ross, I worked only in the Corporate Tax department, calculating tax for companies and complex partnership schemes. The personal tax department, dealing with real people, was way up in the top of the building. Very pleasant and knowledgeable people, who had not the charisma, opportunity or wish to set up in practice on their own, staffed it. A Mr Wardle, whose office was in the topmost attic, headed them. I imagined he was a robust individual, such as the Mr. Wardle in Charles Dickens's *Pickwick Papers*, but I was wrong: he was a very amiable old gentleman such as Dickens's character might have become in his dotage. On both occasions that I needed to take papers from the Corporate Tax department I found him putting aside, as I entered his room, a book of Masonic ritual, which I recognised from my own father having a copy. He was clearly learning rituals in the firm's time, but then, being the most senior partner up there, he could do so.

One very interesting tax scheme I came across while at Touche Ross was being pursued by one of the managers in the same office named Mr Daly. His wife was a breeder o dogs and spent a lot of money on their prize bitch. The animal cost a staggering amount to maintain and then it would lie fallow. Mr Daly spotted an excellent tax opportunity and set up a beneficial partnership for the couple by which she was to receive a small salary plus or minus a small share of the profits or losses and he was then entitled to the bulk of the profits or losses on which therefore there was no tax for her to pay. In fact there never were any profits. In accordance with their partnership agreement he got almost the whole of the loss allowed against his Touche Ross salary, the result being a significant PAYE rebate, while her small share of the losses was set against her partnership salary. I resolved there and then to watch for an opportunity to run this scheme myself one day whenever I could.

In those days the Inland Revenue treated a partnership as a taxable unit for deciding how much of the profit (or loss) was attribute to each partner. Tax on on-going business was assessed for up to two years after profits were earned. The first year was repeatedly taxed in second and third years, unless an election was made fore the second and third year to be taxed on actual profits.

There were further elections about the penultimate two years when the partnership always ceased and restarted when a partner retired or was newly appointed, but for tax purposes one could elect for continuation of the pre-existing business. These elections for star, finish and continuation had persisted since 1920, I believe. One could save vast sums of tax if properly advised. Derek would visit the partnerships to glean details of likely profits, changes in partners and dates of their retirement or admission. He would speak personally, for half an hour or so, with each partner to learn his circumstances as regards tax relief and other sources of income and whether any of these involved loss claims for perhaps, a private woodland or wife's trading venture, which could be offset in a year of choice. Some partners would have affixed salary in addition to a percentage of profits/losses, while others had no fixed salary.

One of the tax tasks we had at Touche Ross & Co. was to look after the Australian Estates Co. Ltd. The chairman of the company was Sir Denys Lowson Bart who we were told, had been Lord Mayor of the City of London in the hear of the coronation of HM Queen Elizabeth II. I later discovered this was not quite accurate it was 1950-51, the year of the British Exhibition. He was duly created baronet, as were all Lord Mayors of the City of London in those days. Upon his death his son, Ian inherited the baronetcy as the second baronet.

The Lowson family owned Estates House on the corner of Gresham Street and Old Jury. They had leased the first tow floors to a Greek shipping magnate and ran their own affairs on the upper floors. Sir Denys had bought a two-storey coffee house on this site several years earlier and had redeveloped it as a six-storey office block, which is not difficult to arrange when you are an alderman of the City. One day I arrived to work on their company tax and noticed a large wooden frieze about 110 inches long by 25 inches high, resting on the floor of our audit room. Nobody knew anything about it but we all agreed that it must have taken some woodcarver months of work to achieve so much detail. We could count thirty-one carved characters. The principal one was a leader on horseback riding on the scene at the left. Next was a small figure of Neptune with a trident and the main central character was a crowned king being burned on a pyre holding up a vast cloud of smoke. On the right was a bare-footed man sitting on a throne and directing that scene. It had the word mahogany crossed out and oak substituted. We decided that the carving did not appear to be Australian, and then got on with our work.

Midway through the morning Ian brought in a man from Sotheby's who briefly examined this frieze, saw the word *Firenze* on the perimeter, and said, "Oh yes! Florentine; early 19th century, but we haven't got that type of sale coming up." They left the room and Ian reappeared later asking if anyone would make an offer for this carved frieze. There was dead silence but I said off-handedly, "I'll offer you a pound for it, Ian." He shrugged his shoulders and left the room, returning half an hour later with an invoice for the carving priced at £1 and asked me to remove it at the weekend by using a certain bell code at the caretaker's door. Obviously nobody else had made a bid for it. "Please can you collect it on Saturday evening between 7pm and 8pm by ringing the caretaker's doorbell? He will have brought it down for you to collect from the ground floor foyer." The carving was only just light enough for two people to carry.

As the day wore on, I realised that the logistics of its collection and storage would be quite a challenge. I was still living at home and Mother refused to give it house room even if I hid it in the roof space.

I was acting voluntarily as an assistant with the local scout troop at the time. Our scoutmaster was the only person I knew who had a strong roof rack on his car, a Vauxhall Velox, and he said that he could be free that Saturday evening. We decided that we could temporarily hide the carving in the roof space of the scout hut and not tell anyone. This mission was accomplished and the carving lay under piles of ropes for about three years until my parents moved to Warlingham in 1973 and I bought the house from them. The scoutmaster and I retrieved the carving, carried it through the streets of Croydon and stood it in my house. I have had the artefact fixed to a wall wherever I have subsequently lived. It is my one trophy from my sixteen years in the City.

Touche Ross & Co. was the auditor of The Australian Estates Co. Ltd. It fell to me to prepare its British tax calculations for two or three years. As it was an Overseas Trading Company there was a problem. It was entitled to some relief based upon changes in British tax laws from some years previously. There was apparently only one Revenue tax manager at Touche Ross & Co. acquainted with how to manipulate this relief. He provided a schedule for me to insert in the annual tax computation and the figure for reducing the deferred tax relief in the Balance Sheet of Assets. It was agreed that there was no point in training up any new staff to deal with this unusual case as it had concerned only a very few companies for just a few years. I believe that the Inland Revenue were equally ill acquainted with this backwater legislation as no one ever questioned the special claim for this Overseas Trading Company relief. The Touche Ross auditors worked on the fifth floor of Estates House and when there was tax work to be done I was established in the room allocated to them.

When I had moved up from the junior to the senior school in September 1959, I found myself every Monday afternoon in a platoon in the Combined Cadet Force where our drill sergeant was Jim Kemble, a senior boy four years older than us. He was demanding yet fair with the powerful voice of an NCO, a task which he took most seriously and competently. I remember that many of us enjoyed the square-bashing and he soon trained us new recruits to a very high standard. I felt that we would all have been proud to have marched straight off to the trenches if there had been a national emergency.

After our school years Jim and I became lifelong friends. We met again, in 1971 at The Golden Lion in St James', London. The Old Boys' Association used to congregate there on the first Wednesday evening of each month. These meetings were informal and usually chaired by John Keene, who had left the school in 1930. One day in 1971 I received a letter from him asking me to accept a place on the club committee. Andy Rutherford had retired after 23 years, and he asked me to take his place, which I did.

Two years later, after nearly four years at Touche Ross & Co. I mentioned to Jim that Maurice Thomsett had arrogantly asked me to look for a new job. It was then 1973 and he had just taken up a new job as group secretary to the companies owned by Mr James Goldsmith and they were forming their own corporate tax department. I adopted Jim's suggestion to go for an interview at one of Mr Goldsmith's offices, the head office of the former Lipton's and Home & Colonial grocery groups in the City Road. I was interviewed by Ken Richards, who was 42 years of age and had been the inspector in charge of Neath 2nd Tax District. He had been chosen by Mr Goldsmith as the brightest of District Tax Inspectors, who were forsaking tax collecting to become better paid as tax advisers, to join his private enterprise. Ken Richards offered me a job but the start date in the Goldsmith's tax department would depend on offices being procured in the City. In fact the job began five months later in September in plush offices in Leadenhall Street.

Ken had been born in Penrhiwceiber in South Glamorgan and would speak fluent Welsh to his wife on the telephone when he did not wish us to know, in our adjacent open-plan offices, what he was saying. He was 15 years older than me and if only I could have got my head around corporate tax, we would have got on well.

There was also an older gentleman accountant, Ken Waites. For many years he had singlehandedly run the tax department at Lipton's and Home & Colonial and had only a short time to go until he would be able to retire at the age of 65. Some of his old friends had got wind of certain corporate tactics being pursued by James Goldsmith. They were concerned about the security of the pension fund to which Ken Waites had contributed for his entire career. Ken Richards was sympathetic and I believe that he arranged for a small enhancement of Ken Waites' pension such that he was able to retire without misgivings. As the time of his retirement approached Ken Waites had taken on an extraordinarily bright and well-informed successor, Bill Benstead.

Two months after the Goldsmith's interview Maurice Thomsett at Touche Ross summoned me to his office. He haughtily asked if I had yet found a new job, not knowing that I had already heard of the planned opportunity in Jimmy's group of companies. I think he was hoping that I would simply hand in my notice to Touche Ross and leave. Unfortunately for me, I still had three months to wait for the new job to start. During that time he became ever haughtier when he spoke to me. However, when I eventually told him that I was going to work for James Goldsmith's companies he suddenly sweetened, so I interjected, "Don't concern yourself. Mr Goldsmith has already examined such firms as yours and has decided to place his empire in the hands of Price Waterhouse." Maurice Thomsett's face dropped as if he had lost some game or other.

PART THREE

WHILE WORKING
AT JAMES GOLDSMITH

IN THE 1920s there stood in the City of London, close to the
corner where Old Jewry joins Gresham Street, an old and very
popular two-storey coffee house. It was bought by a young City
entrepreneur, Denys Lowson, who redeveloped the site as a six-
storey office block, which he named Estates House. From the
upper storeys of the building he controlled his various business
enterprises which included some extensive farming interests in
Australia. They traded under the name of The Australian Estates
Co. Ltd. In the 1930s, the first and second storeys of the block
were the headquarters of a Greek shipping magnate. He came to
be an embarrassment, for he was to be pursued by the police for
some irregularity with his trading empire. However, he was never
taken to court, partly because of complications connected with
the outbreak of the Second World War but mainly on account of
his very poor health. Indeed, he died during the war.

I confess that during my sixteen years working in the City
of London, I developed a fondness for its ancient streets and
churches. I availed myself of a modern edition of John Stow's
Survey of London first written in 1596 and read it at least twice.
Sometime in the 1970s I enrolled for a course of lectures run by
the City Corporation in the lecture rooms in one of the paved
courts set back behind Fleet Street.

One evening each week a group of City aficionados would
assemble for a lecture given by our pansophic course organiser
or by a dignitary such as the City Recorder. At the end of the
course we were told that there would be an exam with a specialist
question on one of five particular City churches. I did not have

time to study all five but happily the particular question was about St Helen's Bishopsgate, which I had indeed studied and admired.

I recall that at the outset there were ninety-seven people in the class. I was very pleased to learn that I had done quite well among the seventy candidates who had stayed the full course. Five ladies, professional tour guides who showed visitors the historic parts of the City, took the top places. I was proud to go to the Corporation office to collect my smart City of London enamel badge.

We were invited to become Freemen of the City of London. This involved finding a 'City Father' to sponsor one, and it so happened that I knew Sir Robin Gillett, baronet, as he was a director of the insurance company which James Goldsmith had acquired. He had served as Mayor of the City for 1976 77. I went to see him in his office at Wigham-Richardson & Poland Ltd, in the Minories, where we chatted about the course while he signed the sponsorship papers. I then went round to the Corporation Office near the Guildhall, paid the £5 required by the Freemen's School at Ashtead in Surrey, and swore an oath of allegiance before one of the Corporation's officers. He had briefly donned a ceremonial dress for the occasion. I came away with the formal papers of a Freeman of the City of London, which many centuries ago would have been a most important achievement for a City trader but nowadays had almost no significance. By a strange coincidence one of Sir Robin's sons, a very talented singer, became a client of mine at about the same time. It was some years before he found out that I had briefly met his father for that sponsorship.

Jimmy Goldsmith's companies included the Cavenham Food Group, Anglo-Continental Bank, Argyle Securities property group and the Wigham-Richardson & Poland Insurance group. There were also a number of others picked up in a blaze of small company take-overs including some bakers, confectioners, and so on. It sounded good to me.

James Goldsmith was an opportunist businessman whose special ability was to identify companies which had failed to optimise their assets. At the time, there was guidance from the

Institute of Chartered Accountants that companies could add 1% compound to the value of their properties in the balance sheet each year without a formal re-evaluation. This concept was long outdated.

Many towns had family-owned department stores which might have been established in Victorian days. Retiring directors had to agree a value of their office property with new directors in order to value their shares and extract their capital value. James Goldsmith relished examining the balance sheets of quoted companies, studying what properties they held and guessing their value if there was no indication of a revaluation having been recorded. I particularly remember his buying shares in Liptons, the nationwide grocers, which had already absorbed the renowned Home & Colonial group of grocery stores. They hadn't revalued the stores since 1957 and high street property values had increased by more than 1% per annum in the subsequent fourteen years. He took a handful of these shops at opposite ends of England, engaged valuers to suggest their true market worth and reached a likely value of all these outlets uplifted in the same ratio. This created a huge capital reserve in the accounts and, as he had managed to purchase the majority of the shares, he declared to himself a £26,000,000 dividend from the company. He repeated this exercise with the celebrated department store named Chiesmans in Lewisham, another public quoted company which did not reflect the true value of its large store in its accounts. I was heavily engaged on working out the capital gain of each property above its 1957 value. It was in this manner that James Goldsmith built up his empire with rather little help from other people. It was not illegal. Anyone could have bought shares in a chain of high street shops that had not been valued for a long time and, on having gained a majority shareholding, proceeded to revalue them and extract wealth in the same way.

Mr Goldsmith, or Jimmy as we came to know him, would repeat the exercise all over the country with small biscuit manufacturers, etc. No independent brand was safe from him.

Names like Vye & Sons as well as Peglers stores were absorbed into Jimmy's vast grocery business.

I saw nothing objectionable in this. Anyone could slowly have bought the shares in the various food or property companies that he targeted. The result was that every company of this kind in the country quickly revalued their properties and declared this high value in their accounts. This made a lot of small investors wealthy through the higher price of their shares, which were then considered safe from a bid from James Goldsmith.

Jimmy had finally established the tax department, right next to his own suite in Leadenhall Street. When I joined the company in September 1973, my first major task was to work out the capital gains taxes on the remarkable number of tiny grocery stores, and a few old supermarkets, that had been sold into Goldsmith's property company (without their trade) in 1971. They had, for the most part, been in the balance sheet at their 1957 valuation for 14 years, eight of which conveniently predated the scope of capital gains tax. Jimmy's aim was to establish the gain for rollover and it absorbed much of my time for a great many weeks.

My colleague Bill Benstead double-checked my figures and the Revenue accepted them all without question as rollover relief stopped them getting any tax on the transaction.

From time to time I would be taken off these tasks to look after Jimmy's group of Wigham-Richardson insurance companies, and then to negotiate its annual tax with the Revenue. This got me away from Jimmy's office and I found that I enjoyed the company of the far more cordial group of insurance accountants.

Lunch at Jimmy Goldsmith's office was a formal affair in the low-ceilinged basement. There were plenty of women who would come in while their children were at school, put on a black dress and lace apron and earn 'a few bob' acting as waitresses. After a year of eating with the same bunch of colleagues 'à la carte' topics of conversation were frankly boring and I for one was delighted when given an extremely generous handful of luncheon vouchers to go and have a quick lunch at a café and then roam the streets of the East End. Once I caught a train from Fenchurch Street to Stepney East (Limehouse) and walked back through what were then the run-down streets of Shardwell and Whitechapel, but every Friday I would walk the full length of Petticoat Lane, listening to the Cockney stallholders. I seldom found anything I wanted to buy but I now treasure the sounds and bustle of Friday lunchtime in Petticoat Lane. One side of Sidney Street, backing on to Petticoat Lane, had been left standing amid much redevelopment. This was to add a touch of reality to the celebrated 'siege of Sidney Street', which I believe was staged before 1910. In another street nearby the façade of another building proclaimed 'Bath House1846'. On the other side of the Whitechapel Road work was in hand in restoring Wilton's Music Hall, which is now a heritage building. There was plenty to listen to and behold from a past era, far more interesting than lunching with colleagues who were nervous of each other.

Three years later, I would be working on a catalogue of 9.5mm home movies, in which I was one of the few people in the country to still have an interest. Ken Richards was content for me to busy myself in this task in office hours when I had completed what had been reduced to 1½ hours' work per day. Jimmy had changed direction in that he was no longer acquiring companies that might require lots of tax attention.

The National Film Archive, part of the British Film Institute, had given me £1,500 towards this project. Together with another film buff I spent some of the money on trips to Paris, where the 9.5mm gauge had been introduced in 1922. I also paid some to Ken Richards' junior typist, who was similarly under-employed.

In 1969 my parents, Ruby and Tom, moved from Ruislip to Croydon and again in 1973 across Surrey to Warlingham. By then I had already accumulated sufficient savings to buy their detached Croydon house.

They had taken me on their first foreign holiday in 1953, when Dad bought a second-hand 9.5mm home movie camera with a stock of film to capture the occasion. Despite the recognised superiority of 9.5mm over 8mm it was poorly marketed and by the 1950s the processing had become appalling. Eventually 8mm reigned supreme and all commercial 9.5mm activity ceased by 1963, even in its homeland France. Finding, collecting and cataloguing 9.5mm second-hand films became my hobby. In 1978 I joined forces with another 9.5mm buff, David Wyatt, and together we embarked on the 9.5mm Vintage Film Encyclopaedia. This occupied us for one evening each week at the British Film Institute library until 1984, by which time we had achieved a most remarkable catalogue with an index of personalities cross-referenced to all the 9.5mm films in various language editions in which they had appeared or worked, all of which were cross-referenced to the original title and date of the film. At its outset David Francis, the curator of the Archive, said that the Institute did not have sufficient funds to produce our work in book form, while his deputy, Clyde Jeavans, said that every effort should be made by the Institute to publish the book. When David Francis moved to an appointment at the American Film Institute, Clyde Jeavans succeeded him as curator and we had great hopes that he would get our book published by the British Film Institute. However, he said he could no longer support the publication, without giving a credible reason. David Wyatt and I set aside the draught book for 29 years whereupon Patrick Mouels, another 9.5mm film buff whom I had known since 1968, revived the task and is now digitalising it. There is hope yet! At all stages we had the full support of Kevin Brownlow, the principal guru of 9.5mm research since the 1950s. I used to relish going to the British film Institute's library each Monday evening after working at Jimmy's, digging out lost details about films long forgotten on 9.5mm gauge. It was a good therapy after work in the City.

* * *

At Jimmy's office, the tax department at its peak would have six tax technicians plus two secretaries, headed by Ken Richards. I would find myself doing masses of capital gains tax computations for Vye & Sons, Liptons, Home & Colonial, Peglers and similar famous high-street grocers. They were grocery shops that Jimmy had closed down in favour of building supermarkets for various other Argyle Securities properties. However, as regards Wigham-Richardson & Poland group I did the entire tax work myself.

From time to time the government would ask Jimmy Goldsmith for sound business advice. Eventually he was rewarded for his services. However, one of the papers got the wrong end of the stick, believing a peerage had been conferred on him. They thought they had a scoop and printed the headline "Lord Goldsmith". In fact he was only knighted!

One day word circulated in the office that Jimmy was to appear in a live television interview in a current affairs programme late that Friday evening. After my parents moved away there was no television in the house but on Fridays I used to spend the late evening with clients who lived two or three streets away. They were very happy to tune into this programme, and we were delighted! Jimmy was being interviewed live by a presenter who had apparently spoken ill of him some days earlier. Jimmy handled the presenter magnificently, soon taking charge of the interview and demanding why he had wrongly criticised him previously. The presenter was reduced to spluttering and for years after, videos of the interview were shown to businessmen "being trained to cope with the media". We were very proud of our boss, being careful to say nothing more than "Good morning, sir" when we passed him in a corridor. Jimmy was very keen that a particular politician should not be elected to parliament and therefore he stood against him in a safe Conservative constituency in Kensington. However, Jimmy did not make much of a dent in the man's expected majority. He did, however, take advantage of the limelight to lambast the politician on live television.

Jimmy decided to start a magazine called *Now!* and engaged an office full of journalists set up in Liptons' old headquarters in City Road. However, it only lasted a few weeks before he closed it down, during which time one of the senior journalists was killed in a car crash.

At Touche Ross I had experienced hectic pressure every month but at Jimmy's it was more enjoyable and less stressful as we were only under pressure at times when the half-year and final accounts were being prepared. On Ken Richards' advice Jimmy based less and less of his 'empire' in the UK, so that by 1978 we were clearly underemployed.

One day, Ken Richards announced to the tax department that he was suffering a hiatus hernia and that Jimmy had arranged for him to be treated within walking distance of the office at the London Hospital in Whitechapel. The operation was a success and we would go one at a time in the afternoons to sit by his bedside as he made his recovery. I was quite alarmed to find that after I had returned from my visit I felt physically drained for several hours. It is not an experience I have had since nor wish to endure again. I had heard of this happening to some people and thought it untrue, but to experience it myself was quite worrying for a while.

One of my office colleagues, Colin, had a brother who needed a serious operation for which the best surgeon worked in Edinburgh. Colin asked if he could take time off to accompany his brother on the night train to Edinburgh and stay if needed to see him settled at the hospital. Ken Richards obviously explained the problem to Jimmy, who asked Colin to come to him in his office across the building. Colin returned to his desk explaining that Jimmy had put his private jet and a nurse at Heathrow Airport at Colin's disposal, at no cost to himself. Colin had only to get his brother to the area reserved for executive's jet at Heathrow Airport, and all else would be taken care of. As far as I know the urgent operation was a success.

The media are quick to chastise leaders of industry but incidents of charity such as this seem not to get given media coverage. It is not something that I could ever imagine happening in my three previous employments in the City.

I took pride in the work on the tax affairs of the enormous Wigham insurance group, but the way Price Waterhouse, Jimmy's auditors, required the information to be summarised was not straightforward. The company's accountants, who were in Barking, needed accounts to be prepared for each company whether or not it was dormant or abroad. I devised my own system for each of the companies in the group so that by following the same template, the accountants at Barking knew where they would find the tax data that they needed.

They were delighted but Price Waterhouse was not happy, even though my work on each company and in summarising them was correct and logical for non-tax accountants to comprehend. Each year, Price Waterhouse sent along a different auditor for the tax. The accountants at Barking never saw the same Price Waterhouse team for two consecutive years while I was a permanent feature for seven years. Price Waterhouse looked upon me as a maverick and it was not easy to convert my accurate summary of tax in to their obtuse standard format.

Of course, we all knew how large professional firms worked. An aspiring accountant would be recruited to the large firms, while on an accountancy course at university. A young recruit's aim would be to build up a curriculum vitae naming the big firms for which he or she had worked. At that time one of these firms, the US-based Arthur Anderson & Co., had a reputation for asking its staff to work long hours into the evenings and weekends. It was prestigious to have been trained in the company. However, during the 1990s the American part of the company was hit by a scandal involving a very serious accounting impropriety, the results of which reverberated for many months across the western world, even hitting the headlines in media broadcasts. Young accountants everywhere realised it was politic to delete any reference to Arthur Anderson & Co. from their curriculum vitae. Such a fall from grace stunned the business community and I was very glad that I had not been one of its whizz-kids!

By now I had spent two years at Hardcastle's, three years at

Longcrofts' and four years at Touche Ross, after which, by moving to Goldsmith's, I had left employment in 'the profession' and was now entered in the world of commerce. For the next seven years I found the ambience of the two completely different.

A great deal of time is spent by almost all City workers in their daily commute to and from home. In my case it was always by rail, be it over ground or underground. With very few exceptions I found that the rail systems always worked reliably for me.

In 1964'65 when my parents lived in Datchet there was only one choice, the Southern Railway from Datchet to Waterloo and thence by miniature tube train known as 'The Drain' under the river Thames to Bank Station.

In 1965 to 1969 when we lived in Ruislip there were three choices. Firstly there was the Metropolitan Line, as eulogised by Sir John Betjeman, which ran through Rayners Lane all the way to Moorgate, secondly by changing at Rayners lane to the Piccadilly Line, which crossed central London and terminated in Hertfordshire. Thirdly there was the Central underground line to West Ruislip which could convey me all the way to Bank Station rather slowly. So in those days, wherever I worked in London there was usually an underground train from Ruislip that would get me close to my place of work. A walk of twenty minutes, through the quiet suburb of Ruislip, would place me at the best station for the three routes to wherever my employer required me to work.

In 1969 my mother bought us a house in South Croydon after my father was told that his civil service job in Holborn was moving to the Whitgift Centre in Croydon. This transpired to be the last nine years of his career. The house that my mother chose was a moderately sized detached house built in 1935 just 200 yards from Coombe Road Station. This was part of the former South East and Chatham rail network running from Selsdon to Charing Cross and Cannon Street in London via Elmers End and London Bridge. I usually travelled on the 07.54 hrs to Cannon Street taking 32 minutes, and returned on the 17.40 hrs or (changing at Elmers

End) the 18.38 hrs. However, if I was staying in London for the evening I would travel back, on the London Brighton & South Coast lines, from Victoria or (by changing at London Bridge) from Charing Cross. Season tickets from Croydon would cover any route to and from Coombe Road, South or East Croydon. The latter was only twenty minutes' walk from home. This flexibility was very acceptable, especially when the railwaymen's strikes did not affect both the South East & Chatham and the London Brighton & South Coast lines simultaneously. The line through Coombe Road was closed down in the week that Margaret Thatcher won a General Election and became the Conservatives' Prime Minister. After that I would walk twelve minutes to South Croydon station or twenty minutes to East Croydon station to reach the other termini.

For my first couple of years the South East & Chatham crews were still running a double-decker train. This had been an extraordinary experiment by the Southern Railways designer Mr H.A.V. Bulleid. This unusual train consisted of a driver's cab and a guard's compartment, then five downstairs and four upstairs compartments with ladder connections. Next there were two carriages with seven downstairs and six upstairs compartments, and the last single carriage was similar to the first carriage but lacking a guard's compartment. The next four carriages were a mirror image of the first four.

This eight-carriage train had a seating capacity that was 1,104 passengers and very odd it looked compared to other trains. It proved to be a total failure because it took so long for the greater number of passengers to get on and off through the fewer doors. Consequently it took longer and longer for the train to reach its destination, thereby delaying subsequent trains. It was a great pity that British Rail had not foreseen how long 'dwell time' at each station would be when they were designing this experimental train. I met an elderly rail observer who was a close neighbour of mine in South Croydon who had several connections with the industry (or he may have been a rail manager, though I never enquired).

He explained that it took an extra half-minute of dwell-time at each suburban station to load and unload passengers through the fewer doors and it took an extra minute in dwelling at London Bridge. "Therefore," he summed up, "after serving five suburban stations it would have used up the pathings of two trains and it would have been just as effective to run two extra trains with normal pathing requirements as the double-decker train." I was beginning to admire the way the peak hour timetables had been pieced together. Puzzled time-hardened commuters on London Bridge station would marvel at this train, thinking it might have arrived from the continent!

When this experimental train was finally withdrawn never again were there ladders or stairs inside carriages. This extraordinary eight-coach train only persists as an irritating memory in most elderly commuters' minds.

As we walked homewards from Coombe Road station one evening, I remarked to my neighbour how intricate were the operations around London Bridge on the South East & Chatham lines. The signallers had to get Cannon Street trains leaving London Bridge to cross safely in front of trains from Charing Cross, at the flat-laid Borough Market Junction. He told me that there was nothing that the signallers in the Cannon Street signal box (which overlooked Borough Market Junction then) enjoyed more than to have a backlog of delayed trains to be cleared. These signallers were adept at clearing eight trains every five minutes. A train frogged across in front of an oncoming service every 75 seconds, but it was done by visual clearance. They could override the track circuit system, provided there was no fog. He explained that when the signaller had seen the roof of the rear carriage clear the points that divide Cannon Street trains from Charing Cross trains he would open the track circuit. He would not wait for the front of the train to reach the track circuit trigger and activate the points. The trigger could not be activated sooner by trains that were shorter than the ten-carriage maximum. I perceived that visual clearance was of great benefit to delayed commuters.

At London Bridge station these South East & Chatham lines ran through the high level platforms numbered 1 to 6 at London Bridge in order to reach Charing Cross and Cannon Street stations, while the London Brighton and South Coast lines terminated in the low level platforms 8 to 16. Platforms 8 and 9 could be used to terminate South East & Chatham trains in an emergency off-peak time. A very limited number of London Brighton & South Coast trains could run through platforms 1 to 6 but only during off-peak hours.

In those days the morning services on the South East & Chatham lines through London Bridge began with a train from the Hurst Green depot near Dartford and one at 04.14 hrs from Addiscombe. This station was east of East Croydon and these two trains were principally for earlier market workers at Billingsgate Fish Market and Borough Market. One fateful morning, there was pandemonium as the train from Addiscombe derailed as it turned into the last bend towards Cannon Street above Borough Market. The rear two carriages brought ballast and ironwork down from the viaduct into the market below. Happily nobody on the train, or in the street market, was injured but the guard at the back of the train was badly shaken.

My first impression was that the signaller at Cannon Street had assumed the ten-carriage train was only an eight-carriage one. This, my neighbour told me a couple of days later when services were back to normal, was impossible for the signal box was not staffed after the London Bridge re-signalling. The London Bridge re-signalling scheme had begun operations in 1974. Trains into Cannon Street and Charing Cross were disrupted while accident investigators inspected the site. I remember looking at the damaged train from the west before it was removed. For a long time afterwards the iron fence along the trackside was left broken and twisted. We waited ages for an official report in which it was explained that the ninth carriage had risen over a frog, the intersection of two lines (in a diamond), caused by a permanent way linesman having incorrectly inserted a plate under a steel chair.

Where the train had turned right on points a few yards earlier, the carriage rocked as usual and the ninth one rose above the frog. There was no evidence of the driver speeding or being negligent. Since those days a new viaduct has been built. It brings Thameslink trains, running through Farringdon, over Metropolitan Junction, through London Bridge between the South East & Chatham, and the London Brighton & South Coast tracks. They run past the London Shard, erected subsequently on the forecourt of the London Bridge station.

These improvements were made after I moved from South Croydon to Totnes. I had endured London peak-hours journeys for sixteen years from 1964 to 1980. Afterwards I only travelled on off-peak services when essential for the other thirteen years. My business visits to London became infrequent and the last was about 2006, after which I was able to do all of my work by post and telephone.

We commuters suffered a few railworkers' strikes, but never were the tube line and buses simultaneously disrupted. I remember getting to the City on one occasion by catching the 64 bus, from South Croydon to Tooting Broadway Station, and thence by the Northern line tube to Moorgate. Once during a short rail strike, when I spent the day working near Euston, I caught the 68 bus direct between South Croydon and Euston. This took an eternity!

In order to reach Wigham-Poland's insurance offices by Barking station, I had to travel from Fenchurch Street station in the City. Fenchurch Street is the oldest of the London railway termini, and thereby the smallest. There were just four efficiently run platforms, or so they were until one morning in about 1979. I had walked to the station from London Bridge with the intention of catching the next train to Barking. I looked at the departure board, which declared that the next train to Barking was due to leave in nine minutes' time as the 09.00 hrs from platform 2. I looked at platform 2 and saw a train quietly waiting, having disgorged its City commuters a few minutes earlier, so nobody was now on the platform. I walked to the middle of the train, entered a 'toast-rack' compartment, slammed the door firmly shut, as one did in those days and saw that I had the carriage to myself. This was quite usual for a contra-flow service in a peak hour and I sat by the window. Sensing that it had been the quickest nine minutes that I had ever experienced I glanced at my watch and I saw that it was only 08.55 hrs when it departed. I instantly realised that this could not really be the 09.00 hrs train. It was probably what in railway parlance is called 'Empty Carriage Stock', which is over half of the morning commuter trains. It was going to the nearest depot to be cleaned, washed and prepared for running back to Southend-on-Sea in the evening peak hour. We were now beyond the end of the platform, clattering over the frogs and points needed at the throat of every dead-end terminus. I realised the train would reach the depot before it reached Barking. I had to stop the train at a station. The only one was Stepney East. If I pulled the emergency brake now the driver would stop on this throat and put every commuter's journey into the station out of kilter for an hour. Yet I did not wish to end up in the depot, which was sited between Stepney East and Barking, as it would take ages for me to be extracted from it.

Stepney East was set in a rather rundown area, known in Dickensian novels as Ratcliffe and as such was once inhabited by thousands of dockworkers and their families. I applied the emergency brake just as we approached this station, not wishing to overshoot it. I then put my head out of the window and thought that I had timed it perfectly. However, the driver had instantly applied the brake and my carriage door lined up with the ramp a few feet short of the platform. Gingerly I jumped down onto the track and pulled my briefcase out of the compartment down on to the ramp behind me. I glanced forward and saw that the train driver was out on the platform standing arms akimbo and glaring at me. I looked back towards the other end of the train and saw the guard hastening up the trackside towards me. I then looked forward again and saw that the station manager had appeared on the platform and I froze.

I called to the guard, before he got too close, "This train was on the board as the 09.00 hrs to Barking!" He quickly realised what had happened and at once apologised. Of course the station announcer had once again pressed her buttons too early, instead of waiting to see that my train was not in service. Yes, he agreed it was going to the depot and that was where most other misled passengers ended up. He assured me that I had taken the best course of action. He also explained that the 09.00 hrs had been waiting outside Fenchurch Street, to go into platform 2, as soon as this one had left the station.

I said that I was surprised that the train had stopped so quickly, as I had pulled the emergency chain ever so slowly. I expected a gradual halt with all the train in the platform. He explained that the chain merely tells the driver to stop immediately, if it is safe to do so, in other words not straddled over a junction where it might have been at risk to oncoming services. I said that I was impressed. He told me that the 09.00 hrs service would be along for me in a few minutes and assured me that I had not brought the entire network to a halt. Thereupon the driver and guard resumed their positions in the train and took it on to the depot.

The station manager presumably informed the area controller of the details, and he probably had words with the Fenchurch Street station announcer. The driver and guard probably had a good laugh about their bit of excitement when they got to the depot canteen. I hasten to add that this was to be the only occasion on which I put my head above the normal rail routine.

Stepney East has now had its third and fourth platforms reopened as part of the new Docklands Light Railway and the station has been renamed Limehouse. This part of London has been given a new lease of life as part of dockland redevelopment since my years in the City.

Anyone who had bought a rundown property in the old Ratcliffe Highway doubtless would have made a fortune on land values and refurbishing as the new developments continued. As usual I failed to foresee it and gained nothing.

One of my clients in Brighton, who photographed most of the rundown streets of docklands, earned a fortune with his 'then and now' photographs. Some of these were sold for substantial sums to companies whose offices were later built in and around the old streets and docks.

In my days of commuting there were three flat junctions on the south side of the river, namely Metropolitan Junction and the two junctions of the Cannon Street triangle. In early days trains branched off at Metropolitan Junction to go to Ludgate Hill and later the brand new terminus at Holborn Viaduct. They still go to Farringdon, Kings Cross and St Pancras, then northwards through to rural England. The relatively new station of Holborn Viaduct has now been closed and dismantled. Thameslink trains now use Metropolitan Junction and Ludgate Hill to reach Farringdon, etc.

In 1977 an eager vicar, Desmond Tillyer of St Peter's, Eaton Square, had organised a number of musical events for the sesquicentenary of his fine neo-classical church. Their organist had passed many singers my way as clients, and when the honorary position of treasurer to the church fell vacant I agreed to take on the role. I attended vestry meetings with the vicar and two churchwardens. One was a senior leading barrister and the other the farrier at the Royal Mews behind Buckingham Palace.

I soon realised that the diocesan finances were rather chaotic and antiquated. This caused me considerable concern, despite the vicar's attempts at explanation, and I felt that it was wise for me to withdraw after fifteen months. I could have found myself involved in something quite difficult and would probably have got into a muddle. After that I did not have the time, or the inclination, to accept any further requests to do charity work. I continued to attend the occasional concert at St Peter's until 1980 and meet such of my clients as were taking part.

In October 1987 we heard calamitous news. After the first Sunday morning service and while the vicar was having his breakfast an arsonist had set fire to St Peter's church and it was completely gutted.

As the fire brigade attended the blaze the police scrutinised the bystanders. They noticed one man behaving suspiciously and he was apprehended at the scene. He explained that he was against Catholics/'No Popery' and that it was wrong for them to have such an imposing church. What a shame that he did not understand that it was one of the finest buildings of the Church of England (and not Roman Catholic) in London. It had been much loved by a worthy congregation and many organists, choirs and singers for 160 years. At Desmond's request I had asked one of my building surveyor clients, Patrick Mouels, to examine the stonework of St Peter's in 1978 in order to assess the need for repairs. We spent a fascinating morning clambering over the roof. Patrick had not realised how large this parish church was. After his report was presented to the churchwardens, I emphasised that the £2,000,000 insurance cover was quite inadequate but the churchwardens explained that the ecclesiastical insurance company would not insure the church for a higher value. It was rebuilt as a smaller church by 1991, with the vicarage, a house along Eaton Square, now sold and a new vicarage where the east end of the church had been sited, like a phoenix risen from the ashes. The arsonist apologised for mistaking the denomination.

In the same week as that great fire at St Peter's, Eaton Square, a great hurricane struck London and the South of England. At my home in South Croydon two trees fell across the road and two more fell over another nearby. A lot of vehicles, which had negotiated their way past the fallen trees, never got to their destination because of other fallen trees and soon came back.

Opposite my house was a fine brick dwelling, built around 1900. The hurricane blew its splendid 16-cowl red brick chimney over against its steep tiled roof. There it rested, in one large piece, against the undamaged tiles. Behind the houses on that side of the road, a lane which served the garages for the blocks of houses on both its sides was blocked in three places by more fallen trees.

In the nearby Coombe Park was a second world war V2 bomb-crater, whose rim was marked by a circle of trees. Young children used to enjoy sliding down into the crater, which was about 12 feet deep. The gale had left all these trees blown across the crater in a web formation.

I walked into town to see the activity on the London, Brighton and South Coast main railway line. There was no apparent damage to the electric signalling system and a few trains were making their way towards London.

British Rail had quickly set about clearing two of the four tracks to Victoria and two of the four towards London Bridge. The dividing of the routes at Norwood Junction was not affected. A skeleton rail service in and out of the Norwood Depot was already underway and it would stretch further out into Surrey and Sussex as the day progressed. The speed of the clearance of the trees was impressive.

With the disruption I decided to work at home for a couple of days. On the third day I ventured by rail to Fulham and Chelsea where there were still cars in side roads, with their roofs perforated by fallen trees, awaiting removal. Most of the trees having fallen away from the houses, pedestrians were obliged to walk along the roads instead of pavements in the side streets. Those few trees that had fallen against houses rested against their bargeboards, having brought down the gutters.

The memories of the hurricane came back to me on the Christmas Eve of 1999, by which time I was comfortably living in Totnes. As the evening wore on quite a gale was whipped up. Once again my house escaped damage but the wind blowing eastwards, towards Paris, caused an enormous amount of damage, even to Notre Dame Cathedral.

By 1980 I was struggling to squeeze my private work into the two periods of the year when Mr Goldsmith's companies had to be given priority. For the rest of the year, my work in the City was dwindling to 1½ hours' work a day such that my immediate boss, Ken Richards, had been allowing me to pay our junior secretary to help prepare the 9.5mm vintage film encyclopaedia for publication, yet I was still employed full time with the rest of my underworked colleagues.

Eventually Ken Richards broke the news that he must dispense with three of his staff. As one of the chosen ones I was to receive a month's pay for each of my seven years of service with the company. He deeply regretted not being able to find me a new job at Price Waterhouse & Co., Mr Goldsmith's auditors. I had to restrain myself from showing my delight when he broke the news to me.

I imagine that on being made redundant most people are immediately worried about what they might do to get another job. But in my case my private practice income had already surpassed my satisfactory City salary. My clients had known that I was holding down a City job, but when I told them that I was now independent I found myself taking on even more of their colleagues. Indeed, in the year 1984 I was offered 104 new clients, mostly musicians and singers.

I myself had opted to transfer my Touche Ross pension contributions to Mr. Goldsmith's Cavenham Foods pension fund. Touche Ross had arranged their pension fund in such a way that employees leaving could transfer their contributions to their new employer's fund but the contributions Touche Ross had put in the fund for employees could not be transferred. I was quite upset on being told this. It had been explained in the 'small print' that I was not in the fund during the first of my four years. Nonetheless the pension I was to have from age 60 was very satisfactory and unexpectedly amounted to 37% of my closing salary at Jimmy's.

I had worked for seven years to 1980 in Jimmy's tax department, and within three years of leaving my freelance practice reached bursting point. I still recall the amazing feeling of relief when I realised that I would not be part of the daily bustle of commuters and knowing that I would no longer be told to do tasks in a way that I felt was unclear. I had to return my company car within eight months. I seldom used it and let one of my clients in my neighbourhood borrow it, but I had never asked him for any contribution provided he always made the car available when I needed it.

PART FOUR

WORKING ENTIRELY ON MY OWN

U PON LEAVING GOLDSMITH'S I was surprised to be asked to work at Wigham-Richardson & Poland as a freelancer doing what I had been doing for the past seven years. We quibbled about the fee but quickly reached a satisfactory sum and I must say that it was a great relief to be told that my method of summarising the tax was precisely how they wanted the task to be continued regardless of Price Waterhouse's objections. I undertook this assignment for two contented years.

At Touche Ross (1969 73) and at Jimmy's office (1973 80) I had learned that I had no inclination for corporate tax. After fourteen years I was happily helping self-employed individuals and a few partnerships with all their tax problems. They grouped their turnover as freelancer, gave me P60 or P45 annual employment certificates, their deeds of covenant (later known as gift aid), details of their savings/dividends/pension/annuities, etc. They learnt that if they followed my instructions carefully I would quickly do the rest and give them details of what to expect by way of tax liabilities.

At Longcrofts' we used to get lots of questions from the tax office on personal cases. It was excellent training that enabled me to judge how to present the truth to the Inland Revenue in the most efficient way. I had taken my own decision never to employ a clerk who might mess things up. As I was not training up the next generation of tax accountants I'm sure that neither the Institute of Chartered Accountants nor the Institute of Taxation would have approved of my method of office management.

I had learnt much from my Buxton, Beresford & Co.'s

experiences at Longcrofts' such that I only took on clients if they agreed to follow a simple set of instructions. Most clients sent me their accounts by post but it would often be easier for me to go to see them by train. I found that only a few clients needed to be visited, as most had no trouble following my simple instructions about categorising their expenses and such matters. I always took pride in having intelligent clients keen to follow these simple instructions and be aware of their tax obligations.

One of my earliest clients was a pianist for silent vintage films projected at the National Film Theatre on the South Bank. He introduced me to the other pianists and it turned out he was newly qualified at the Trinity College of Music, now Trinity Laban Conservatoire of Music and Dance, and was an outstanding improviser of mood music on the piano. Within a few months he had introduced three of his girlfriends to become clients. However, one of them who had been a music teacher had trouble with her car and put it in for servicing while deciding to go to teach on her bicycle. Unfortunately she had tried to carry her cello on the bicycle and very sadly died from the injuries sustained when she fell off. Another client to die while a client was a highly-strung Irish man who taught guitar and who took his own life in 1977.

The chairman of British Petroleum also became one of my clients. He had arranged with the Vehicle Licensing department that when the suffix 'L' was issued in 1972 He would be able to buy BP 01L as a special favour. He happened to own a magnificent old 1928 Bristol car which was, of course, his pride and joy. As soon as the 'L' was issued, he changed the registration number of his car to read BP OIL and drove in great style from his home in Crowborough to the chairman's parking lot opposite British Petroleum's head office in London and went upstairs to his room to watch everyone who was looking at this fabulous car. Within half an hour, head of security politely came into his room and said " Sir, you can't go round with that number plate on your car; you know you are a target." The end of the episode was that British

Petroleum purchased the number plate from him and put it on one of their delivery lorries. He had had his moment of glory.

He weighed at least twenty stone and suffered from sleep apnoea, having to sleep in an almost upright position at night. One Saturday morning he felt a little unwell and walked over to his doctor's surgery. While waiting to see the doctor he collapsed in the waiting room and died. I was genuinely upset.

National Insurance Contributions matters absorb many needless hours of official time in the various Revenue departments and in offices of accountants across the United Kingdom. Taxes are levied on capital gains and on income, be it earned or unearned. National Insurance is levied by Her Majesty's Revenue and Customs on earnings with exemptions for foreign earnings.

Until 1978 it was relatively straightforward. What was due on employment earnings was collected via the PAYE system that was conceived in 1946. Self-employed people pay their National Insurance direct under a fixed rate known as Class 2 contributions with a surcharge for high earners known as Class 4 contributions. Until the advent of self-assessment a lot of time was wasted in calculating these Class 4 contributions and I often wondered why there was not some merging of them into income tax. There had after all been no Class 4 surcharge before 1978. It seemed fair to charge it but so much of the clerical time was spent by the taxpayer and by tax offices creating and administering these extra rules. In self-assessment we currently have to show a figure of how much Class 4 profits are exempted on account of being earned abroad and other exemptions. Such ramifications are mind-boggling.

Both Class 1 employed earnings and Class 2 have minimum levels below which no contributions are due. Of course, careful employers then formed different companies, each to pay the same staff less than the threshold. The Revenue counteracted this by requiring that all earnings associated with one workplace should be aggregated as one employment. So a group of employers, in identical industries, grouped together to swap workers for part of each week. In that way not all earnings were in the same workplace.

The conception of Class 4 in 1978 was a remedy to the abolition of the short-lived Selective Employment Tax of the mid-1960s but was still too cumbersome. It would have been simple to aggregate self-employed earnings with earnings in employment, deduct foreign earnings, deduct a threshold, and levy a rate on a scale of rates up to a maximum contribution, charging it all in one go to the taxpayer instead of his various employers.

The Labour Government's Minister of Pensions and National Insurance, Mrs Barbara Castle, went on television to promise to simplify the system but this proved to be yet another government promise broken. I recall some of the complications that even now could usefully be simplified.

First we had self-employed people whose accounts for the income tax office would not be accepted by the National Insurance office. Various tax-admissible headings would be dismissed in calculating Class 2. It was not until the 1980s that the National Insurance office realised they could dispense with clerks examining the same accounts for people whose profits were near the Class 2 threshold for liability. Thereafter, they would instead use the same profit figure after deducting capital allowances as the tax office accepted. However, many self-employed people had some portion of their earnings that had suffered Class 1 at source in a part-time employment. These still had to be deducted to calculate whether Class 2 was due on the rest.

At Longcrofts' in 1966, all staff had to add sixpence per quarter hour to their records of time spent on each client in order to cover the cost of the new-fangled Capital Selective Employment Tax. However, this was not reversed when Selective Employment Tax was abolished after a surprisingly short time as being unduly cumbersome. Class 4 was initially set at 4% in 1978 but gradually rose to 8% by the time I retired.

The assessment to Class 4 was on the same profits being assessed to income tax for that year. Most of my clients ran accounts to 10th April near the start of that year. This meant that all self-employed persons were assessed to tax on accounts ended in the previous tax year. That way my clients paid their Class 4 on what they had earned over 'two years less five days', having had the benefit of two years of no tax on their initial year of negligible earnings. At the time most of my self-employed clients were musicians of about 25 years of age. As they began to flourish their profits would exceed the prior-year profits on which they were now assessed for income tax. However, the National Insurance offices insisted on their calculations being based on actual profits. This complication was still troublesome when I retired.

An upper limit was decreed for the Class 4 surcharge. The first complication came in needing to apply for its deferment in advance, due to suffering Class 1 on some of the earnings which need not suffer Class 4 as well. For this one had to ensure that the relevant form was received and promptly dealt with, for anyone suffering Class 1 employment. Clients had to tell their accountants if they had started an employment and what they thought their total employment earnings would be. Most musicians had no idea which of their earnings would or would not suffer Class 1 at source. Many were confused and were apprehensive about making their guess excessive. I managed to appease most of them and the Revenue never seemed to worry about sums being 70% inaccurate when guessed in advance. At the outset if Class 4 was deferred, it was wholly deferred. The Revenue realised they were missing out and amended deferment to only partial deferment. Many months after the year was over, a new set of Revenue clerks would try to credit all Class 1 earnings against all Class 4 assessment. In fact, they were deducting current Class 1 earnings against the Class 4 earnings which would have been based on earlier profits when the accounting date was not before 6th April. In my experience this was usually beneficial to my clients. However, after about fifteen years the Revenue ruled that the deduction for Class 1 in the Class 4 calculation should be based on the ingredients of the Class 4 assessment rather than actual earnings in the year of assessment. Because they insisted that they had misinterpreted their own rule they refused to alter calculations of previous years to the same basis. It seemed that everything the Revenue did in this area got it into deeper mire than was intended.

In some complex cases where I perceived a computer mistake and telephoned the National Insurance office, the clerk could not get his head around the confusion. Taxpayers had 28 days in which to understand these calculations. Accountants all over the nation would rack their brains to try to comprehend this paperwork. We could only check it to a limited degree to assure our clients that it seemed to be correct.

I wonder whether the erstwhile Minister of Pensions and National Insurance, Barbara Castle, could ever have simplified all these regulations and calculations during her short term in office, despite her reassuring television announcement that she was going to tackle the issue. Another feature was that we had to ensure that our clients paid 30 years' National Insurance contributions under Class 1 or 2 in order to be assured of their full state retirement pension entitlement. Class 1 brought extra earnings-related pension by dint of the graduated nature of Class 1. Classes 1 and 2 were mutually exclusive in enabling a year to tally for that state pension. Class 3 was a credit system for unemployed people for which I had no experience. Class 4 was a surcharge on higher self-employed earnings in the UK (unless they had borne class 1 at source) and conferred no right to additional state pension at all. I often thought how I would simplify the system if I had been given a chance but every idea produced its own complications for certain earners. Anyway, we had to muddle through with the system that the government operated. It may sound cynical to say that I got the impression that each new government resolved to simplify the system but kept realising that any simplification would temporarily delay the collection of tax or contributions with national cash-flow ramifications. I imagined several reports being written by several government departments, none of which were lucid and comprehensible let alone a solution, such that things just got left as they were with a plethora of staff in an office in Newcastle trying to adjudicate the system. In many cases they had to examine the affairs of many individuals one at a time every year despite a commitment to cut their office staff.

Every accountant is at some time asked to take over work that has been previously entrusted to another. The commonest reasons are retirement of a clerk or partner or exorbitant charges. The latter often occurs because the other firm's partner or accountant has delegated the job to a clerk who is not properly trained or experienced. In making corrections himself the partner has then added a portion of the cost of having to remunerate his faulty clerk as well as himself. It was always frustrating for a partner to find that he had an excellent clerk able to cope with a variety of taxes but unable to get his head around the ramifications of National Insurance. I remember at one stage I had challenged the Newcastle staff on some particular aspect that amounted to a double charge, only to find that their 'technical' department stood it's ground yet two years later admitted that my understanding had been right in the first place. In one case I had forgotten the name of the client involved and in another case my client had retired but did not take up my offer to re-open the case on her behalf.

It always amazed me how many firms did not conduct their initial discussion with clients in a way that appraised them of what was essential and the costs for which they could claim. Many of my clients told other musicians what they put together and what I was able to achieve in a perfectly legal way. I recall that in a four-year period I took on 15 straightforward singers and musicians from a firm in Bedford Row that did not discuss the clients' freelance earnings. In my experience this firm seemed not to contemplate these considerations in their dealings with new singers and musicians, which is why I took over 15 of what to them were relatively new clients.

As my business grew anyone introducing a new client would already have told him or her how important it was to follow the simple procedures that I requested. I emphasised that clients could even ring me at weekends if need be. Anyone who delayed their affairs would get a call or letter from me offering to help.

At any given time I could have more than three hundred clients diligently summarising their annual figures in this way. It proved to be a very effective system, making it possible to prepare accounts and tax returns easily and promptly.

By 1983, fourteen years into my being a chartered accountant, I had already worked for 518 clients and my business was full to bursting point. I was able to direct the potential overflow of my accounts to Raymond Benn, a certified accountant who had offices at Tunbridge Wells. We had first met in about 1976 when he was employed at Jimmy Goldsmith's.

At first we found that some clients left his service after a short while and I suspected that he was not giving them quite such individual attention as myself. It was to be some time before he successfully adopted my style of work. When approached by a new client for whom I had no spare time I would always write down the essential starting details that I would have absorbed myself and suggested such things as length of first accounting period and so on to Raymond.

Two years later a female accountancy graduate from Croydon Technical College came to me and asked if I could help her set up her own business. I agreed and she was quick in learning the rudiments. After a few months she started to have medical and personal problems which affected her business. A few of her clients transferred to me, and I was able to absorb them, but the rest went to Raymond. By then Raymond had got over his teething problems and was progressing well with each new client.

I worked from a long room upstairs in my South Croydon home. A Scots couple with three young daughters came to live next door. The husband had a good job only three miles away. Unfortunately, he soon had to leave his work owing, I understood, to an illness. His physician prescribed jogging but his enthusiasm for it quickly waned. When I announced in 1993 that my girlfriend and I were moving everything down to Devon, the wife exclaimed, "Thank goodness there will be no more clattering of your typewriter throughout the weekends!" I had no idea that when I had the window open my typing could be heard down in their garden and had been an annoyance. I had sold my house to a couple who worked in London. They had a young daughter and I often wondered whether she became one of those girls who relished playing pop music loudly. I knew that my upstairs office would become her room. How might those neighbours react to such a noise as would emanate from her record player now that their own children had grown up?

All my clients knew that I was now fully self-employed, and that I was already working to full capacity, yet new clients kept on coming. After 1984 I took on no new clients except as replacements when another client no longer needed my services. With a few exceptions I was able to concentrate on personal taxation for professional and vocational people.

Some of my new clients came from West End accountants, having received massive bills and yet been given an unsuitable annual accounting date. This had cost them unnecessary taxes in their opening business years and, though I would explain this to them on the telephone, nobody ever tried to get redress.

As soon as it became clear in 1970 that I was going to be asked by many people to work privately for them, I set out a modest charging-rate for all types of work, be it technical or routine, a letter or a phone call, a journey or whatever, and stuck to it. I was definitely not a person to claim extra fees for a successful outcome to a dispute with a tax inspector, as I regarded this as greedy and unprofessional and it would have played on my conscience. For the first decade while I was travelling daily into the City I was on a season ticket and I did not charge fares. Most clients had addresses in London or they could meet me in the Green Room or a church vestry after their professional evening performances.

Some professional firms would quote a range of fees from partners down to clerks. This always confused new clients as they feared that a lot of partner hours might be charged. I am convinced that those firms did themselves no good and I hold that a single charging-rate should be proffered for all work, with the partner not counting hours when he is discussing with his junior work that has been done on that client. Few clients realise that having been charged for the junior doing the work they are charged again for the partner look at what the junior has done and discussing it with him. The more people looking at a taxpayer's affairs, the more expensive it is for a client when all staff time is aggregated. This is why it is important for my type of client not to entrust his affairs to a firm with layers of staff. It is sufficient for one trained person to see a client's affairs through the office each year and thereby be fully acquainted with them. It is very annoying for clients to telephone their accountant's office only to find that a new clerk is on their case and as yet has no knowledge of their business. Clients are always happier when they believe that one person on his or her own is dealing with their case year after year. They always get upset when there is a change of staff for they usually suspect, quite rightly, that there is no longer anyone in the firm who can recall the format and history of their business. The client should be told that this rate would be subject to periodic increments in accordance with inflation. It therefore became no problem to raise the charging-rate by 25% when we suffered that level of inflation during Edward Heath's government of the mid-1970s.

A handful of my clients asked why their fees seemed high in the first year or two. I would explain that they had not carefully followed the letter of guidance which, I had sent to them at the outset. Once they had grasped how they could ease things for me their subsequent fees settled down. Nevertheless, I always ensured that my fee-notes gave a description of each task that I had to perform and how long it had taken, including the long introductory letter of guidance, which for example, categorised their likely admissible expense headings.

Those who took the trouble to read my itemised notes were wont to ask for similar details on bills from other professional advisers such as solicitors. All the work I undertook would be marked up with the time I had spent on it ringed on my working papers so that I knew just how much time I had to charge in my annual fee-note. There was no guesswork. Consequently, it became rare for clients to question a fee-note, as I would draw their attention to the narrative and time shown for each task in the fee-note that they were questioning. It is a pity other firms do not usually itemise their fee-notes with the time spent on each task and its date.

* * *

On reflection, my not having to spend time justifying a less responsible billing system certainly enabled me to have more time for progressing my clients' affairs.

Moreover, by not employing staff, I did not spend time reviewing and even correcting their work. All such reviewing of work by other people in the same office would have been duplicated time for which no charge could be justified.

Like most people, I left the City with memories of many traffic incidents.

Outside the offices of Touche Ross & Co. the streets of London Wall and nearby Moorgate were each bi-directional. However, eastbound London Wall traffic turned northwards along Blomfield Street and then continued eastwards along Liverpool Street. Pedestrians were protected from the traffic by a long line of railings where Blomfield Street turned into Liverpool Street. One lunchtime I emerged from the offices of Touche Ross to find that a young woman had tried to cross the road. She was pinned between a long lorry and the railings on the inside of this corner and was half-conscious and obviously in pain. The police had arrived and one constable had taken up point duty. He was in the middle of Blomfield Street, where there was a turning left into Finsbury Circus, and firmly directing all of the confused motorists to turn left. A police motorcyclist rushed up along the inside of this line of slow-moving traffic. When one motorist turned left, as instructed, he knocked the motorbike to the ground. The result was that the police then had two incidents to resolve, one of their own making!

One evening after a late client meeting I was walking back past Bank to the office and found Princes Street absolutely quiet. A double-decker Regent RT3 bus, at the northbound stop in Princes Street, had its nearside wheels in the gutter as was appropriate. A police car had clearly sped down Moorgate towards it, but misjudged its speed where the Bank of England juts out into Princes Street and driven straight into the offside front wheel of the bus. The police car was a wreck. I did not ask a sombre policeman if there had been a fatality as I feared a positive answer. The police had clearly been evacuated from the smashed car and rushed away in ambulances. What surprised me was that the strong police presence was allowing only pedestrians into Princes Street and not press photographers. The sole damage to the bus appeared to be a puncture to its offside front tyre.

On another day I emerged from a lunchtime recital at Allhallows-on-the-Wall church, which was given by one of my singer clients. As I was coming out afterwards I heard sounds of an accident taking place in Bishopsgate and went to investigate. A chauffeur-driven car had become wedged between a red double-decker Routemaster bus and a lorry coming in the opposite direction. I presumed that some wealthy City magnate had told his chauffeur to dash between the vehicles. The bus driver could only get out of his cab by standing on the roof of the wedged car.

It was a standing joke in the City that Number 11 buses always came in pairs and seldom at steady intervals 'due to catching one another up in dense traffic'. Don't you believe it! The conductors and drivers of the Number 9 and 11 services took their meal break in the bus workers' canteen at Liverpool Street. Some of them ate quickly and some ate slowly so that they could synchronise their departure from the terminus. I clearly remember one day seeing five Number 11s setting off from Liverpool Street in convoy down Old Broad Street towards Bank. Sometimes there would be a mix of 9s and 11s which shared the route through Bank, St Paul's, Fleet Street, Strand and Charing Cross, where Number 9 continued to Mortlake.

* * *

Part of the third-rail electric system of British Rail ran past the bottom of our gardens in South Croydon. It divided us from the back gardens of houses in the road beyond. The station, named Coombe Road three hundred yards away towards London, was useful for me to get to Cannon Street station in the City. However, British Rail began to reduce the service to peak hours and started to cancel even those trains as a preliminary to gaining permission to issue a closure notice. In those days British Rail never hired a replacement bus for these cancelled local services. The closure was on the same day as Margaret Thatcher became Prime Minister, 4th May 1979, and I rode on the final train to Sanderstead station and back.

A few weeks later I walked the abandoned line after the tracks and 11,000-volts power supply cable had been removed. When it was built in late Victorian times the residents of the nearby fine villas on Park Hill insisted the railway line be hidden in dark shallow tunnels. By the year 2000 these old tunnels were once again in use and had become part of the Croydon Tramlink system. New Addington, a 1930s estate built to house displaced London dockers, had waited over sixty years for a promised rail link to Croydon but was now given a superb rapid tram link all the way to Wimbledon as well as Croydon. I had been doubtful about the route shown on the original plans but now felt that no better route and solution to their transport needs could have been devised. Full marks to the planners!

Several of my singer clients had residencies at particular churches, synagogues, cathedrals or abbeys. If they were not at liberty to appoint a deputy when on holiday or absent for another reason, then they would probably be on PAYE as an employee, but if the selection of a deputy were left to them then they would probably be engaged on a freelance basis.

At the time of the crisis about Martin Neary, Master of the Queen's music at Westminster Abbey, some four of the regular choristers were clients of mine and accounted for a third of the total. Martin Neary had been appointed as organist, choirmaster and Master of the Queen's music at the Abbey, and if approached privately he would hire out the choir to film studios without, it became apparent, telling or obtaining the permission of the Abbey authorities.

Somehow, the Dean or other authorities realised what had been going on and Martin Neary was dismissed. He appealed to his ultimate employer, who was Her Majesty the Queen. It instantly became hot news in some newspapers. Somewhere along the line, the Inland Revenue became interested in Mr Neary and opened an investigation into the way his accountant handled his affairs.

In order to corroborate his accounts they found it necessary to ask the choristers for a list of fees earned from Martin Neary, and this was undertaken in the guise of an enquiry into each of the regular choristers' own affairs. They sought the date each fee was received whether from Martin Neary's 'system' or not.

Obviously this involved a lot of work, as I had been content to receive one total figure of fees plus expenses reimbursed from each engager. The question quickly arose as to who was to pay for my and the other accountants' fees, given that the enquiries were instigated solely because of each chorister's innocent engagement with Martin Neary. The Abbey accountant replied to my question, saying that the Abbey would pay the extra costs direct to each chorister. I explained that this would be a "benefit in kind" and taxable under PAYE on each chorister, so that he would be out of pocket by the PAYE and National Insurance charged on the reimbursement, so a further sum would need to be reimbursed to each one. Eventually the Abbey accountant asked me to send an analysis of my extra time charged, plus one invoice for the lot. The Abbey paid it promptly and all parties were happy. I understand

Mr Neary was in deep trouble and had to seek work in another country.

There was no issue about Martin Neary's musicianship. He was undoubtedly the right man for the job but was not safe if left to organise his own affairs for the British tax authorities.

I was later told that he had similarly hijacked the choir at his previous cathedral appointment in England, but the Inland Revenue were not involved, although they had power to enquire into such past work if fraud were now involved; this seemed unlikely.

The incident was stressful for the innocent choristers at the Abbey, but none of them had missed fees or shown the Revenue anything other than competence and honesty in their tax dealings. One of the choristers had brought a P45 to the Abbey which showed he had to pay no PAYE tax at his previous employment and the Abbey continued with the tax code as instructed by the Revenue. He was worried that the Revenue might realise he should not have a 'No Tax' code at the Abbey and alter this code. Probably due to an oversight in the sheer volume of the investigations the code was left and he continued to be treated as a freelance at the Abbey.

I met my close lady friend in 1990 and in the next year we bought a house in Totnes in Devon. I finally moved my business there in 1993 as it had been delayed because there was a property recession and because my estate agent had pitched the sale price far too high. I am very proud that in the move only one file was lost. It was the one on which I was working when the removal men finally arrived. Luckily it was one I had only recently started.

I read, in the Institute Handbook that Jim Calver-Jones had moved from Longcrofts' to practice in Cheltenham. I telephoned him on 13th January 1994 to say that it was 25 years to the day since he had given me my first client, from which I had quickly built up a sole practice. He sounded rather sullen about my genuine gratitude. For many years I had no idea that he had had to leave Longcrofts' with some ill will. He deserved better than that.

After I had settled into my final office in Totnes I spent an hour in totalling my business turnover derived from working in Croydon. I discovered that it came to just over one million pounds. For twelve of those twenty-four Croydon years I had also received a satisfactory salary in the City of London.

I then reflected on my aforesaid neighbours in Croydon. The wife had had to get a job as a schoolteacher to support the three daughters and her incapacitated husband. He went jogging less and less often and seemed to rest at home. He could have jogged to Croydon Technical College and retrained to earn a living like most heads of families. After all, his sight, speech and mobility seemed sound and he did not appear to be suffering from depression. He too could have clattered a typewriter and gained a sense of personal achievement like mine. I felt it was so hard on his wife to do all of the breadwinning.

No career as long as mine could pass without some notable milestones of disputes with the Inland Revenue. They included some disappointments, some successes, even some victories, and sometimes I enjoyed seeing the Revenue shoot itself in the foot.

I recall dining, some thirty years ago, with a journalist who had attended the same school as me. He wondered why accountants had secretaries to type their letters. I explained that when working for myself I always typed all my letters and accounts. It was unusual for me to draught a letter, as I found it very easy to type letters as I composed them. Therefore I never needed a secretary to be involved in my letter writing which would have required my having to stop and read what she had typed, which I would have seen as time wasted. On hearing this he implied that I was working like a journalist. I commented that not all accountants have the ability to think ahead in the way they write letters or plan clients' affairs.

Avoiding interruptions where possible is the key to the efficiency of an accountant. Disruptions from colleagues and secretaries are usually counter-productive. There was a tradition in many offices which meant that no partner should ever be seen typing. The cost of staff adds huge sums to a firm's expenditure and should be avoided if possible.

I remember noting that several partners at Longcrofts and Touche Ross & Co. were clearly distressed when their personal secretary was away sick or on leave. Some of them had their private secretary clattering away on her machine in the corner of the same office, which I would have regarded as a distraction but which was essential due to the potential cost of an extra office for her and the high office rents in the City.

For my annual holidays in the 1980s I would travel to the South of France by train for a few days rambling among the hills near Briançon followed by a fortnight on the beach at Juan-les-Pins, using the coastal mainline railway to dine in a different restaurant and resort every evening. I had been lucky to find a quiet nine-room family-run hotel called 'La Marjolaine' situated two hundred metres from Juan-les-Pins station and three hundred metres from the endless beach. A few weeks in advance I would have two gross of small labels printed which stated *Fermeture Annuelle* with the dates of absence in French. I was hoping that no would-be burglars noticing such a sticker on my notepaper would understand French. My faith was justified, although it instilled some bemusement among my clients who for the most part did understand French.

I believe that there were only three or four clients who did not like corresponding with me by Royal Mail and who would have preferred to use their computers. I was quite happy to let them find other accountants while I preferred working with the security afforded by Royal Mail. Nowadays a serious failure in internet security is announced in the media nearly every month, so I am very pleased never to have suffered a leak in client confidentiality. The vast majority of my clients acceded to my own view that they would be happier if their personal tax and wealth details were not shared with online hackers across the world. I emphasised that I truly did not wish to be embroiled in any allegation that a client's personal affairs had been hacked. Sending a copy through the Royal Mail had always proved to be secure and reliable. I recall only two instances of non-delivery of Royal Mail in my 44 years of using our postal service for business and both of these were in London suburbs.

The business affairs of the vast majority of my self-employed clients became routine after their initial years. Unless some fresh feature had to be addressed it was always a relatively simple process. I would usually have their accounts prepared, tax returns filled, all computations completed and the Inland Revenue reaction checked, spread over a total of six hours. It all worked very well as long as things were kept reasonably up to date.

I must confess to having had a tricky time with one London family. The husband was a journalist on a national newspaper and his wife was employed in the St Martin's area of London as a literary editor. When she resigned her employment to have a family I 'cashed in' her P60 for her to recover the surplus PAYE for the partial tax year. When it was realised that their third child had a disability, the husband became entirely self-employed and was able to help more with the family. In about 1990 she resumed her work as a literary editor, albeit as a freelance. I lodged her initial accounts with St Martin's District Tax Office, using her old St Martin's tax reference. After six months I had a call from a confused tax office clerk complaining that her tax reference number made no sense in their system. I said that my letter had explained that my client was one of St Martin's former taxpayers who was coming back into the tax system and that she needed a tax return.

I heard no more and we received no tax return so I continued to prepare the accounts each year and put them in duplicate in my filing system ready to be sent to a tax inspector when one replied to me. Having had no reply by 2002 I agreed with the couple that I would make a clear note on her husband's tax return, using words to the effect "My wife has sent you her accounts but you have still not sent her a tax return". This was repeated the next year and again no notice was taken of it. So in 2004 I asked her to countersign the same note and in 2005 we repeated this countersignature procedure.

The following year she received a letter from the tax office suggesting that she had a source of income and should be filing a tax return. I wrote, with attached accounts, which showed the previous profits awaiting assessment from 1990 onwards. The inspector accused us of withholding information about a source of income but I was able to refer to our 1990 correspondence to the old St Martin's District Office. It had since been closed when the Revenue merged a great many of the tax centres. I sent him copies of the correspondence but he refused to believe that I had ever sent the top copies and accounts.

Eventually the Complaints Office to whom I had appealed agreed to look for the husband's tax returns, on which I had put the annual note about his wife's source of income. The complaints inspector had to accept that her signature was a valid declaration of income. He then raised six years' assessments and charged interest from the dates that the tax thereon should have been paid. However, he did not make any assessment on the twelve years that were out of date. The tax saved roughly equalled my fees in arguing the case and the said interest and no penalty was charged. I realised too late that I should have requested the clerk's name and the file reference when I was first telephoned in 1991. I had of course expected him to follow up the papers and issue tax returns at once.

Accountants who act for musicians and singers need to know that there is a group of tax cases which determine whether someone is freelance (and thus able to claim a great variety of expenses in whole or in part, but excluding entertaining costs) or employed (with only a little chance of claiming some expenses). It may be necessary to enquire as to whether the musician or singer who hopes to be treated as a freelancer can appoint his or her own deputy when unavailable, whether there is a pension scheme, whether he or she is available to other engagers, and so on.

Here I recall a trombonist who had a residency in a West

End show. It meant that he was allowed to put in a deputy to avoid playing the same score six times a week. He was wont to switch between such musicals with another trombonist, who had a similar residency at another musical show. They both undertook some teaching of children on Saturday mornings so that the next generation of talented musicians would be well trained in Local Authority music centres. At great cost he had bought himself a new instrument but in the following year the show had closed down. A three-partner West End firm of accountants advised all of the stage staff and orchestral players that they would receive tax-free compensation for the loss of their jobs. The firm made the unfortunate mistake of not restricting their assurance to those people who were on PAYE as employees. They seemed unaware of the *Van der Burgh's* tax case of 1927 which ruled that the tax-free status only extends to freelancers if the work had been the vast majority of his or her freelance earnings. All of the orchestral players were freelancers with plenty of other similar engagements each year. By applying this case none of them was legally allowed to exclude the lump sum compensation from their freelance accounts. I advised them to refer back to the three-partner firm who eventually admitted that their advice to musicians with freelance status at the particular West End show was quite incorrect and applied only to the employed (PAYE) staff at this theatre. My trombonist was delighted that I had averted what could have been an enquiry and said that the other musicians on the show were grateful not to have been pitched into a time-wasting argument if their tax inspector were alert.

Many of my clients did not know that several of their colleagues were already clients of mine and it amused me when I discovered that this trombonist was waxing lyrical about my having saved him from trouble had their compensation not been included in this income. It was only when he warned other musicians of this pitfall that he found he was talking to others of my clients! What surprised me was that a handful of clients told me that I had intervened and rescued several musicians from certain trouble. Obviously I felt quite chuffed about this and I told them that small firms often excelled above large firms who lacked the relevant specialist!

Back in the 1970s tax inspectors were plentiful and they asked petty questions which were usually resolved with one letter of my answers. Then came the announcement that the Inland Revenue tax office staff would be reduced from 66,000 to 55,000. I soon noticed that some of their minor rulings were quite wrong in law, indicating a lowering of their training standards. Gradually I found that the number of minor questions and enquiries that I received were reduced to less than one a year spread across over three hundred active clients' cases.

In the late 1990s the Revenue decided that in many cases, depending on turnover, they no longer wished to see annual accounts. It is not possible to estimate the loss to the tax system in wrongful claims for expenses and the temptation to miscalculate taxable turnover. I deliberately ignored the temptation not to submit accounts with each client's tax return and I know that this unnecessary procedure averted most of the remaining opportunities for questioning because tax inspectors would glance at the unrequested accounts and realise that questions would be pointless.

There used to be a lot of fuss about freelancers not being able to claim the costs of meals against tax unless they were a part of an overnight hotel bill. Eventually accountants running their firm's PAYE payrolls discovered that the Revenue's Inspectors themselves who were coming on premises to check the PAYE system were receiving an untaxed meal allowance, instead of catching the bus back to their office to the canteen for lunch and then returning for the afternoon. Accountants were aghast! A great fuss arose as to why this did not apply to everyone whether freelance or employed when working away from the office. Eventually the Inland Revenue took the wise decision to allow a reasonable tax-free meal allowance depending on hours away from their business base, thereby scotching the many victorious decisions which they had acclaimed against freelance taxpayers in many previous decades. Accordingly I put a new heading reference into the accounts each year, '*Caillebotte v. Quinn (1975) setaside*', and explained to my clients in their first year, that it was the ultimate case by which these meal allowances had been argued and disallowed. Many forgot and did not begin claiming it. Where this was obvious I telephoned the client to say they had not heeded this major alleviation of so strong a previous rule.

If I identified such forgetful clients I would telephone for a cash estimate if I could locate them and remind them that the reason why I had so many headings of expenses in the accounts was to enable them to glance through the headings in the typed accounts every year and to check that there was no heading for which they had forgotten to claim their costs. Otherwise I would point it out in a letter after their accounts were prepared.

I remember that just after the 'setaside' was introduced, another firm rang me and asked what was my authority for asserting that the rigid tax case denying meal costs had been set aside? I explained that I made a point of having an evening dinner at a Croydon restaurant with an old school colleague who had become a senior tax inspector and was entrusted with a succession of three or four London District offices. He had been bemused by some of the complaints that I had sent to his offices, as I had not realised that he was their man in charge until he had revealed his identity to me at an old boys' dinner of my old school one year. He told me a lot about the Revenue organisation in those days and under Chatham House Rules I was able to tell him a lot about how we were trained in accountants' offices.

At our Christmas dinner in 1997 he told me that he had been on one of the senior tax inspectors' training courses at Bootle. His lecturer had explained that inspectors should no longer reject claims for reasonable meal allowances when freelancers were working away from their normal place of business. This was a complete reversal of the *Caillebotte v. Quinn* principle. This was a tax regulation where it is deemed that the cost of food or drink, taken in whole or in part for sustenance, was not allowable. At this stage the Revenue had not published the 'setaside' to taxpayers and the tax profession and judging by the number of calls I received from other firms expressing their incredulity it would seem that I was 'ahead of the game' in telling my clients that the Revenue were no longer applying the *Caillebotte v. Quinn* principle except where they had found a taxpayer being untoward in his tax claims. It was some years before the 'setaside' became law but I always dreaded what the tax case had cost Mr Caillebotte as it worked its way up through the courts to the ultimate House of Lords decision in 1975.

One day I received a telephone call from a clerk in the Institute of Chartered Accountants protesting that I had not a sufficient Continuing Professional Education score, a result of their looking at my entries on the Institute's annual return for practitioners. I told him that I had this annual one-to-one Christmas dinner with a senior tax inspector who would talk liberally about developments in personal tax legislation and administration whereby we would swap knowledge and experience on a broad scale. I asked him how I could claim this in my score and what rating his department would assign to it. He was baffled, probably because he had never come across a chartered accountant privileged in having such annual *tête-à-têtes*; his instruction manual clearly couldn't cope with it! Anyway, he was content with my explanation and did not want me to change my ways. The Institute never challenged me on Continuing Professional Education again!

One of the great tax schemes that I learned at Touche Ross had been the successful dog breeder scheme which Mr Daly had run in partnership with his wife. In my subsequent career I was able to use this scheme several times for various types of trades. The most lucrative was indeed in another dog breeding partnership incurring a succession of annual losses. The Revenue never raised any questions yet each year they automatically issued PAYE repayments to the higher earner, one of my successful musician clients who had a mixture of freelance music and PAYE work. Until my retirement I really relished the various schemes that I could operate with partnerships. I was always amazed at how often a prize bitch could lie fallow and gain his master massive PAYE refunds!

As the years passed there were many other occasions when I saw partnership tax opportunities for my musician clients. Typically there would be a change of partner in a group of singers with a new singer joining. He would have had scarcely any earnings on leaving Music College. I would visit them to explain that there could be an adjustment to current profits for those of almost two years ago when profits had been leaner. This was unless a 'continuation election' had been signed by all and the partners or their legal representatives (and lodged at the tax office within the prescribed two-year time limit for validity). Such continuation would mean that the more lucrative profits would be heaped upon the new member. It was still tax-free as his allowances, otherwise unused, were claimed against the income of two years previously. The outgoing partner then found that his final profits were reduced to previously expected tax. It was easier to explain the overall reduced tax on fully declared profits when I did the accounts of every partner.

The main difficulty was finding new partners whose accountants did not understand the tax rules and the ramifications. They would continue to insist on showing actual profit instead of taxable profit on the tax return. When these problems were overcome many people wondered how I had legitimately achieved such low taxes for them. I explained that I had had the privilege of being well taught by a fine tax partner named Derek Chapman at Touche Ross & Co., whose practical expertise and planning far exceeded anything that one could learn on an H. Foulkes Lynch course.

Not every one of my clients took or could take my advice. I recall a school in Chelsea which was founded and run by the same man for over 50 years. Although his son, an outstanding musician, and his daughter-in-law were set to succeed him he refused to share the profits with them and no hint that I gave to him or the son was heeded. The existing school accountants wished to incorporate from the moment of death and that was that. I felt really sorry that those accountants had not seen what to me was the obvious partnership scheme which should have been operating.

Contrast this with a major firm of architects based in Central London with accountants in Clerkenwell. One partner who was due to retire was very unhappy about his tax affairs. He came to me on the advice of his secretary's husband who was one of my musician clients. Faced with the architect's accounts for the three years and with the expected profits for the current I was able to present a scheme. If they made a continuation election new partners would use up more basic-rate tax and outgoing partners would save far more. It also caught the eye of the senior partner who saw the overall and his own tax reduced. I had only to explain that the scheme made legal use of the new partners' unused standard rate tax bands. A month later the architects offered me the entire partnership tax task to work upon but I had to decline it as I now had a full clientele. By now, my general experience was that looking after a partnership was like looking after four more clients than just the partners. I proposed that I could spend time teaching their accountants the special advantages of partnership tax that I had learned from Derek Chapman of Touche Ross & Co. but my suggestion came to nothing.

I am quite sure that there were hundreds of partnership changes every year where there was no partnership tax expert on hand to guide them to consider making a partnership continuation election as opposed to a partnership cessation and recommencement if using an annual accounting date after 5th April.

In 1986 the Revenue finally changed the rules from 'almost two years' to 'almost one year's arrears' and much of the scope for elections, etc. disappeared. I had learned the best way to deal with sole-practitioners' tax from James Calver-Jones of Longcrofts'. I had left him in 1969 some months after I took on the first of my private clients. Thereafter it was Derek Chapman who would teach me the intricacies of partnership tax and all of its possibilities and ramifications. To these two men I am deeply indebted for imparting their knowledge and giving me practical experience in areas that I would work in so often in the following 40 years. I do not doubt that Gerald Bunker's managers or James Calver-Jones could have taught me such schemes but they did not have partnerships as clients. That which Gerald Bunker and James Calver-Jones did not teach me at Longcrofts', namely partnerships, Derek Chapman certainly did. This was to be the most interesting and worthwhile part of my training and I am hugely indebted to Derek Chapman for selecting me to work on the detailed partnership tax in 1970 and 1971. Derek's remit was to advise three or four stockbroker partnerships whether they should incorporate when the Stock Exchange Council relaxed the rule that firms had to be partnerships and therefore responsible for their own business losses if any were incurred.

All aspiring chartered accountants were enrolled in correspondence courses such as in my case with H. Foulkes Lynch & Co. At the approach of professional examinations firms of chartered accountants would send their juniors away on revision courses, often six weeks long and run by such firms as had been managing their correspondence courses. Course work specific to partnership tax schemes was almost negligible. However, we all benefited from each other's alert questions to the competent lecturers and of course we made lifelong friends.

On my first refresher course I had found myself seated next to a young lad whose middle initials were 'de W'. I asked him whether I could make a guess at his middle name. With sheer confidence he said yes. I said that I thought it was de Winton. He was aghast! He asked how on earth I had guessed it. I said I had once read a book about the Brecon & Merthyr railway and remembered that the principal local bankers in Brecon who financed the railway were the nineteenth century de Winton's' Bank. He said that there was a most convoluted Trust that no lawyer had been able to unravel since the nineteenth century and that everyone in the family had de Winton as their legal middle name in case somebody one day sorted out the frightful mess and did not recognise the beneficiaries. He had not actually travelled on the Brecon & Merthyr railway before it succumbed to Dr Beeching's closures in 1963, and I said the most exciting rail journey I had ever enjoyed was with a large group of boisterous Merthyr residents who travelled every summer Saturday evening from Pant to Brecon returning at twilight on the Saturday special from Brecon through the oldest (1816) railway tunnel in the British system. This was followed by the longest steep railway incline at Glyn Colwyn (6½ miles at 1 in 37) with it's magnificent large reservoir and fishing facilities, through the sharply curved eighty-eight degree tunnel at the top into the highest railway station open on the British Railways network named Torpantau, 1,314 feet above sea level, that was quite an exhilarating 14-mile journey in boisterous company. I added that we had not called at the half-way station, Pentir Rhiw in Glyn Colwyn, as all the fishermen, who were the only people who ever used the station, had gone home on the previous train and probably relished the peace and quiet on that earlier service.

During my career most of my disputes with the Revenue centred on the *Salisbury House Estates Ltd v Fry* (1930) tax case. The Revenue was very keen to apply it and while it usually worked in their favour there were a few notable cases when it did not. Clients seldom understood the fuss that I made on their behalf but they seemed satisfied that I was able to play the Revenue at its own game.

One client in this situation was a freelance violinist. She found herself performing more and more concerts for one of the BBC orchestras and eventually she was put onto their payroll as an employee. She had worked in previous years for the BBC. By dint of that *Salisbury* tax case her previous year's BBC fees could not be included in her accounts because by the time these 10th April accounts came to be taxable, the BBC work was PAYE (Schedule

E) and no longer freelance (Schedule D). So I applied the *Salisbury* principle and then she therefore had the benefit of two years of fees at the BBC being tax-free and was of course delighted! After another two years they made her a permanently employed orchestral member yet again.

The *Salisbury* ruling is clear in asserting that one cannot be assessed on prior years' freelance fees (Schedule D) in the same year as the same work is changed to being a PAYE employment, and it is the Schedule D freelance sums that tax inspectors automatically agree to exclude when their attention is drawn to the same source of income potentially being taxed simultaneously under Schedule D as well as Schedule E. The phrase one always needs to quote to any confused tax inspector is 'the Schedules are mutually exclusive'. Unfortunately, I found myself having to explain this to other tax accountants via their clients who had been protesting that their tax had been 'bundled up' like a 'double whammy' in a single year. Therefore you cannot assess under Schedule D something that you insist on assessing as Schedule E in the same year. To which I once received the response "No, all these BBC orchestral musicians must be assessed under Schedule E", which often meant they shot themselves in the foot when the musician came off contract in order perhaps to join a group of musicians with a less demanding work schedule such that the occasional BBC work once again became freelance. Given the recurrence of this situation with a number of musicians, I often wonder how many other accountants press the point about the *Salisbury* case and get a year's fees freed from tax each time.

In 1977, a couple of journalists who worked for the BBC asked if I would help one of their colleagues. He had come from the USSR to work for the BBC's Russian Service at Bush House, the grand office block sited between Aldwych and Strand in London. He prepared programmes on cultural topics such as London theatre productions and needed to account for his freelance income to the Inland Revenue. I found that he had kept no receipts for his taxis and theatre tickets, etc. and I had to emphasise to him the importance of such evidence. Nonetheless we estimated the expenses and I prepared his accounts which the Inland Revenue accepted without question.

The next year there were again no receipts. Yet again the Inland Revenue raised no questions, let alone requests for vouchers. For a second time I made clear the necessity of proofs of payment for expenses claimed. When for a third year there were still no vouchers I advised him that I could no longer act professionally on his behalf. I told him that if the Revenue were to ask to examine his accounts and I could not furnish them with the supporting material, my entire business would be put under suspicion and I could not jeopardise the smooth running of my more responsible clients' affairs in that way. I presume that he must have found another accountant. The two clients who had introduced him to me explained that Russians were deeply suspicious of their authorities. He probably could not adjust to the generally frank approach that prevails in the United Kingdom.

Throughout my career I had clients from such countries as France, Germany, Sri Lanka and the United States of America, all of whom shared the British approach, and thankfully I had no more clients approach me from Russia. I mention this in case any aspiring British accountants think that it is safe to deal with the Russians on their own terms with their innate belief that fabricated figures are OK in Britain!

I had to have a general policy of not taking over clients whose affairs had been steered into a muddle by other firms. However, I did take on work from clients of a firm in Bedford Row where I found that for the most part they had been allocated an unhelpful annual accounting date. The 15 clients who had switched to me from that firm had 5th April or 31st March as their annual accounting date. I was rather proud to say how fortunate it was that I had reviewed their affairs and changed them to 10th April straightaway, thereby delaying, by almost a year, the year-on-year extra tax due as their earnings increased.

There was always a risk that a large tax bill might come at

cessation but this only happened with two clients. In 1987, when the Revenue changed the assessable basis period, we were given an almost unbelievable relief or let-out arrangement by which three years (less five days) were all averaged to form one single year. This unexpected facility was like manna from heaven. It was difficult to explain to clients that a couple of years would not be fully assessed to tax. I proudly looked upon the wisdom in having chosen 10th April instead of 5th April or 31st March as the annual accounting date, and pitied clients who were still stuck on accounts dates late in the tax year such as 31st March or 5th April, rather than a date early in the tax year such as 10th April. Even when I retired clients would be saying to me I never understood why my accounts have to run to10th April yet everything else in the tax return has to run to 5th April. I would offer to list the profits made in each year against the list of profits taxed but warned them it would only show a large and legitimate saving in tax throughout their careers.

Some readers may already know that until the 1980s professional accounting practitioners were allowed to recommend insurance and assurance companies to their clients. They would also accept commissions in doing so and there was no obligation to declare it to their clients. The professional institutes merely expected the practitioners to act in the best interests of their clients, a vague requirement open to a host of interpretations. Some professional accounting partnerships might delegate one of their number to see which property and chattel insurance or life assurance companies would offer the greatest first-year commission. Sole practitioners were more likely to peruse performance charts in their professional magazines and then contact the local agency office of the best performers without regard to the commission offered.

In my own case I listened to three elderly clients, who had done better than they expected with Guardian Financial Services (formerly Guardian Royal Exchange) policies. I checked them out as satisfactory on the charts in my professional magazine before introducing myself at the local agency office in Croydon. It was within walking distance of my office at home.

One of the first tasks undertaken by a recently qualified musician or other professional after appointing an accountant may be to seek a mortgage. He or she would need to furnish figures of earnings for the mortgage application. Many practitioners recommended that a client should at this stage have an endowment mortgage even before he or she has settled with spouse or child who would benefit at the client's death. My advice was to forgo the 15% life assurance premium relief on such a policy, not yet needed, and to opt for insuring his or her life for the term of, and amount of, the mortgage, but when we discovered how cheap these premiums were many clients took my advice to insure their lives to age 63 for two or three times the amount of their first mortgage. Despite the greater number of years covered, the full-life benefit was still rather cheap. I persuaded the Guardian Assurance Company to put into the assurance contract a phrase that the sum assured should be paid even if the policyholder had not died by age 63. I asked the manager of the local Guardian office whether this could be a standard feature for all the clients I would introduce to him. After words with his head office he reported that they were content to put this 'live or die' phrase into the quotation sent to the clients and myself. In about 1988 there was a change in legislation and the Guardian ceased to provide these term assurance policies for which there had been a most agreeable 100% tax relief on the premium given at the clients' highest tax rate. Clients who had assured their lives only for the amount of the mortgage frequently asked for an additional policy to cover any future mortgages. Up to 1988 I sold ninety of these Guardian 'term assurance' policies. One client, a musician who played early string instruments, died as a young alcoholic during the term of his mortgage. I advised his family to ensure that his executor collected the policy proceeds. It transpired that he had changed banks without transferring his Standing Order. Over thirteen months had passed since the last premium payment and the company, quite rightly, refused to pay out the vast death benefit due to him.

Nevertheless, several mortgage lenders belittled this type of cover. They urged clients to have mortgage endowment policies which would pay out only if the client died during the term of the mortgage.

Following the establishing of the Financial Services Authority (FSA) accountancy practitioners had to register if they were to sell, or advise on, assurance products. I signed up for six years until I became despondent with all the red tape and bureaucracy. My practice, whereby one half of all commission on 'sales' of assurance products was credited to my clients against my fee-notes for time spent on their affairs, was not accepted as good practice. I had effectively been operating this procedure for almost twenty years until I was told I was remiss. I was not showing why I only sold products offered by just two companies, The Guardian and The London and Manchester assurance companies. Upon this challenge I ceased all new assurance policy activity.

Some months later the Guardian refused to send me the renewal commission to which they had previously stated that I was truly entitled. Worse was to come in that many years later the Guardian sent notice to my relevant clients that the "whether you live or die" clause included in their policies was invalid as regards clients who survived the term of their assured mortgage. One by one each of these clients protested to me. Every time, I sent a complaint to the Financial Services Authority. In every single case they found in favour of the client, whereupon the Guardian offered to convert the policy to an endowment with the same term of years at no extra premium.

On each occasion an official at the financial Services Authority would ring me up to check the details, notwithstanding my having already sent with our submission a copy of the quotation showing the words 'whether you live or die'. I pointed out to the FSA official who had telephoned me that it was this clause that had induced my client to proceed with the policy. The initial quotation stated, "Provided all premiums are paid", and allowed the Guardian to make two increments in premium within a certain restricted percentage.

This was more cosmetic than practical as the Guardian was collecting all of the premiums by direct debit, thus ensuring that all increments took effect. At one point I recognised that the same official had dealt with three of these identical complaints. I told her that the Guardian's refuting the 'whether you live or die' clause in the initial quotation was getting a little 'déjà vu'. She explained that every time a complaint was made to the Authority, the Assurance Company had to pay them an administration fee. It was obvious to me that the Guardian could not flag up the words 'whether you live or die' in a policy and thereby save itself the vast administration fees by conceding to the client's appeal when first made. The FSA agreed that the Guardian was behaving oddly in referring each individual complaint to the Authority, given that it would always cost them this administration fee. She realised that in every case the FSA was directing the Guardian to restate their policy. It had yet to accept that the 'whether you live or die' assurance quoted must be honoured in full. I began to suspect that the Guardian's system was unable to register this 'agreed' deviation of 'whether you live or die' from their standard policy.

I was more than a little upset that the Guardian had welched on its agreement but pleased that it had got its 'come-uppance' from the Authority. None of my clients lost out. Needless to say I was very proud of having insisted on the insertion of this clause at the inception of each policy so many years earlier. I felt that I should have been trusted to carry on selling policies without formal regulation. It made me wonder how many other agents might have insisted on such a clause before entrusting their clients to insurance companies who had offered these pre-1988 term assurance policies.

Nevertheless, there was one former client who lodged a complaint to the Guardian that I had, as he put it, 'mis-sold' him this policy. He had already been a source of much trouble to me. When not making much headway with his freelance career as a musician in London he had moved to Cornwall into what seemed to be an employment. Anyway, the Guardian sent me his address on the copy of his complaint and I contacted him. I told him that I would gladly show him how to get the Guardian to honour their obligation if he would at least settle my final fee note sent to him in London many years earlier. Sadly he never paid my fee and presumably the Guardian never paid out a vast sum on the policy to which they had firmly committed themselves. He did not understand that he had carried on living past the date on which the policy would pay out the assured sum whether he lived or died. Sadly there are some people you try to help who just do not understand what you tell them. I never received my outstanding fees from him and he never noticed the 'whether you live or die' deviation from their standard policy. The case was closed. Amongst the ninety 'takers' there may have been other policyholders in this unfortunate situation after leaving my clientele, in the great number of years between quotation and the end of the time assured. Nonetheless, I hope that they may have shown the original quotation to their subsequent financial adviser, though I suspect not.

Never before had I been so glad that I had kept every old file from the start of my business in 1969, and I was very glad to have photocopied and saved the Guardian's quotations. It had been set out on 'No Carbon Required' paper and therefore was fading even though it was kept shut in the dark of a closed file. Despite this 'nasty trick' played on my policyholders by the Guardian Financial Services, the company's policies continued to perform satisfactorily. My own financial adviser, whom I had lately appointed, told me that the Legal and General tended to achieve better results in later years.

One day it occurred to me that there might be other clients entitled to some proceeds of Guardian policies. In the late 1970s, one of my clients was a particularly talented professor of music.

He had an allocation of highly gifted organ pupils at a London music college and was also the organist with a fine adult choir at a prestigious Belgravia church, St Peter's, Eaton Square. Sadly, after the Sunday service of Eucharist, he would dive into a pub with some of his choristers and over-indulge. His long-suffering wife, Rosemary, was kept waiting to serve their roast dinner, the one meal that she relished preparing each weekend, and it was nearly always over-cooked. Unsurprisingly she left him.

He then befriended a mezzo-soprano, Laura, who after the conflagration at St Peter's lured him from his London drinking friends to a northern city where again there was a notable music institution and a prestigious church with a fine organ. One night after she had gone to bed he returned inebriated to their home and she heard him roll down the stairs in the dark to his death. Laura telephoned to tell me of that sad event and a couple of days later I recalled I had set up a life policy for Peter from which Rosemary was supposed to have benefited. Anyway, I rang Laura back and asked if she had collected policy proceeds from the Guardian amounting to several thousand pounds. She had not and I recommended she send probate to the Guardian with the policy number which I read to her, telling her that I had not yet billed her late husband for my most recent work. She kept me informed and was very pleased that the Guardian recognised her claim and sent her a sum equal to what had been her husband's previous mortgage. Of course she was very grateful.

It was so distressing that this popular tutor, with all his joie de vivre and acclaimed talent, had to die in such circumstances. Nonetheless I remain grateful to him as he introduced so many choristers and organists to me as clients. They all survived me into retirement.

There are undoubtedly many people unaware that their partners have old life policies, often dating from before their marriage, which they have never mentioned. Many widows may throw away their husband's papers without perusing them. This is another way in which life assurance companies can make such remarkable profits.

When the Institute of Chartered Accountants invited me to take part in a survey of firms to report the efficiency of staff, etc. with statistics, one of the scrutineers rang me. He asked how I had managed to charge out 1,754 hours that I reported for a year as asked in the sample. I said it was not a mistake as I worked at home and so had little or no travelling time, I had taken nine days off for Christmas and 22 days off for a summer holiday in the South of France as usual at Juan-les-Pins. I did not need to waste time engaging staff, which gave me a very calm and satisfying life. He remained amazed when I assured him that I had perfected a level of efficiency with which I was comfortable to work stress-free. I looked at the results of the survey but realised that not many firms like mine had bothered to take part. I rather felt that voluntary surveys are pointless because only a small and atypical group of members get involved. So the whole survey was, like so many others, a complete waste of time.

Accountants are frequently called upon to conduct time and motion studies. I believe that my clients were capable of forming their own judgement as to whether to employ a secretary, to have other office staff, and just where to use computers and e-mails, etc. In my initial letter I asked them to list precisely the details that I would need in my preparing their accounts and income tax return. I emphasised that provided they omitted nothing then it should not be necessary for them to visit me on business. Consequently, if they did come down to my part of Devon it would often be to go for a ramble across the countryside that I so much love or perhaps we would have a meal and get to know each other socially. If there were to be any hesitation at my invitation I would declare that the clock had stopped running and that the meal was on me.

Once I had left the City to work solely from my home in South Croydon, my business trips into the heart of London became weekly rather than daily ventures. I had developed my business largely as a telephonic and postal one with no clerical help. I relished being able to think immediately of a client's detailed affairs as soon as they might telephone me. This was very much the one-to-one discussion that clients wanted as they could not benefit from discussions with clerks or partners about their business affairs as they would not know to whom to speak. I could always judge when a client was entirely happy with advice in an impromptu telephonic discussion. I could see it was a major load off their minds. By the time I moved from South Croydon to Totnes my visits to the heart of London were very much reduced and such trips as I made to London allowed me to work for up to three hours on the train if necessary. From Totnes trains either went to the north via Birmingham or to London. I could change from a London train at Westbury or Reading to go to South Coast stations. There was no more struggling through London from one terminus to another for an onward journey. For example, Totnes to York was a no-change journey.

When I first moved to Totnes there were four or five trains a day to Birmingham and beyond and six to London Paddington. From about 2002 this rose to about ten to London and beyond and an hourly clock-face timetable north to Newcastle, starting earlier and finishing later in the day. This vast improvement in the service may have resulted in a major rise in Totnes house prices. The London housing shortage led to a significant number of people keeping a bedroom in the metropolis, to which they commuted late on Sunday afternoons, returning late on Friday afternoons. The three-hour Totnes to Birmingham or Totnes to London service on Sundays and Fridays means that people are doing a five-and-a-half-day week while people in their homes in London are still doing five-day weeks because of being with their family every evening and weekend. People who use their cars to commute long distances to their weekly workplace are only able to do four-and-a-half-days' work if they choose to avoid the Friday evening rush back to their family homes in the countryside. Good examples of this phenomenon are the excellent rail service from South Devon direct to leading cities compared with people living along the dismantled railway between Senny Bridge, Brecon, Talgarth, Hay-on-Wye, Ross-on-Wye and Gloucester.

The reprivatisation of the railways in the mid-1990s evoked a greed for profits to placate the new railway entrepreneurs, with blatant disregard for their customers the passengers. Train operators had to pay the train owners for the mileage per carriage which was run. The managing director of the company which operated the London trains to and from Devon and Cornwall decided to remove the seventh carriage from many of the eight-carriage trains, without adjusting the seat reservation system. The result was that on a number of occasions I found passengers from Plymouth wandering up and down the train trying to find the ticket examiner, only to be told that their reserved seat was in the missing carriage.

Another of the so-called economies was to reduce the level of maintenance on the locomotives so that heavy-duty tasks were performed less frequently. This led to several instances of trains breaking down while in service, often deep in the countryside. The company had already cut the number of locomotives held ready to retrieve a floundered train. Often a push from the train behind was organised but would prove to be ineffective if the couplings did not match. In every case, when a passenger train had pushed the one in front, it too had to be taken out of service for examination by engineers in accordance with a stringent rule. Eventually the travelling public rebelled and demanded an inquiry that reported a worse state than had been feared. Promises were made, the managing director was retired prematurely, and there were a couple of new short-lived appointments. By about 2004 the right man for the job, Mark Hopwood, was appointed.

The operator of the trains to Birmingham and beyond introduced a slightly inferior fleet of trains. For two or three years they kept breaking down all over the network. However, when these teething difficulties were surmounted they ran efficiently and it was easy to learn the hourly clock-face timetable by heart. Typical was the problem encountered in foul weather south of Dawlish station. This track was originally built by Isambard Brunel's design by Peter Marjory, an outstanding twenty-five-year-old railway construction engineer. The high waves were directed up the battered sea wall to be turned over on themselves, thereby keeping seawater off the track, but after those men retired, and this track was twinned in 1900, a fresh sea wall which did not direct the high waves back over themselves was built out on the beach because residents of Marine Parade in Dawlish would not allow the Great Western Railway to build additional track on the land side. The result was, as everyone knows today, that storm water rushes up the 1900 sea wall and falls on the top of trains. The trains designed in the 1990s for the cross-country route from Devon to Birmingham and Scotland were built with electrical apparatus mounted on their roofs which immediately short-circuited in storms and brought all services to a standstill. It was quite some time before the roof design of these new trains could be modified for 'Dawlish storms'. There is also a slow-moving geological fault just north of Dawlish station which causes different problems. Various promises to build an alternative railway have always been shelved and the opportunity to reinforce the track bed with a steel girder bridge north of Dawlish and to adapt the present wall south of Dawlish to deflect storm waves has also been shelved. Meanwhile the sea wall south of Dawlish which satisfactorily deflected storm waves before 1900 lies buried beneath the middle of the twin tracks at that point.

The only disappointment was the removal of profits from the system. This should have been spent on updating the network and reopening lines where populations had now expanded, and the building of more of the superb trains which have given forty years' service already on the London to Penzance route. However, the incentive to new entrepreneurs by which they could pay themselves high fees and withdraw profits has deprived the railway system of the necessary funds to reinvest. In Victorian times the original entrepreneurs were able to reinvest in expansion and improvement but this is not undertaken to any significant degree these days for fear of the government re-nationalising the railways with very little return to the entrepreneurs. For example, various dismantled track beds should be reinstated. The trains to Newquay should be routed via St Austell and Parkindillack, not via Bugle and St Blazey. Trains from London Paddington to Bedwyn need only four and half miles of track to be re-laid through an old tunnel to reach Marlborough and give that town an hourly service. Trains to Aylesbury could be extended to Brackley in Northamptonshire, trains from Sunderland could be run direct to Durham. Trains from Cardiff to Penarth could be extended to Lavernock and Sully. Trains to Redditch could be extended to Alcester. With the opening of Stansted airport, Haverhill has expanded from a population of 4,500 in 1950 to 26,000 in the present day, but nobody has reinstated the train service through Saffron Walden. Relatively speaking, there are other such quick fixes which would solve problems in particular areas of the country. The railway is also probably the one public utility which should have been improved with hourly clock-face timetables long before re-nationalisation in order to attract the vast number of businessmen and women now using it in preference to overcrowded motorways.

As the years passed, more personalities from radio and television called in than I can remember. They were always rather impressed with my home in Totnes. Hay Hill is only twelve minutes' walk from the train station and four minutes' walk from the top of the town. It has outstanding views of Dartmoor and the Haldon Hill, plus easy access to an A-road at the end of the old carriage drive. Trees muffle the sound of cars which pass within fifty yards of the room that I dedicated as my study.

I gratefully look back on the high professional standards which were instilled in me at the companies for which I worked in the City: first at Hardcastle's, with John Palmer, and then at Longcrofts', where Jim Calver-Jones's enthusiasm for me to grasp personal tax was invaluable. There was also the remarkable work in partnership tax under Derek Chapman at Touche Ross. Finally

I must recall Ken Richards at Goldsmith's for whom I hold much respect. Thanks to my mentors in accountancy, the whole system for my clients worked perfectly from the outset. I could never have foreseen that Jim Calver-Jones' suggestion that I might take on some personal tax clients privately would start me on my 44-year, comfortable and stress-free private career.

As I write this it is 28 years since John, the gardener, began his work here. He came to look after the small woodland set around the 1826 carriage drive which curves up to the house. Now he also cares for our one-third of an acre of garden and lawns which rise to an orchard and small wood, owned by the Woodland Trust. I reckon that the stone walls of Hay Hill give us an extra nine days of warmth each autumn. I truly hope that the next owners will enjoy what has been such a calm environment in which to work and live. All around there are plenty of quiet country lanes for rambling. Living here has been the happiest time of my life.

PART FIVE

KIBBLEWHITE VERSUS COMMISSIONERS OF INLAND REVENUE

I T MAY BE true that every long-serving tax practitioner cherishes an achievement in his career with special fondness. Sometimes it might be a tax scheme which has been accepted by the Inland Revenue and which he helped to formulate. At other times it may be a procedure which one has seen work time and again and which legitimately saves a client from paying excessive income tax. Much can be achieved by presenting the figures in one way rather than in another. All we tax accountants are experienced in many such schemes without the need to omit or falsify figures.

The case that gave me the most satisfaction in my career was that of Michael Kibblewhite in 1981/2, because I could not convince the tax inspector on a point of fact.

Mr Kibblewhite was a talented musician and conductor who worked with four or five amateur choirs as their guiding light. He would prepare and conduct their rehearsals, and many of their performances, and he was also a guest conductor at the invitation of other choirs. Most of his work was carried out within forty miles of his north London home. I already had a few such talented conductors as clients. I realised that where the source of funds for a choir came from a Local Education Authority I had had no trouble establishing their freelance vocational status for income tax. This was despite some earlier case law to the contrary, inferring that it was an employment.

At the start of Mr Kibblewhite's career the tax inspector had looked closely at the structure of his accounts and ruled that he was employed by each choir and should be taxed on PAYE. This meant that very few of his expenses would be accepted against tax. However, if he were taxed as a freelance conductor, they would all have been allowed. In addition to this 'choir rehearsal' employment he sometimes received a fee for conducting their public performances if they were not having a guest conductor. The inspector argued that if he conducted these performances it was an extension of his employment with that choir. I had argued that as the job did not mention the conducting of performances, these fees were like all the guest fees he earned with other choirs, which were undisputedly freelance fees.

My client was aware of other choral conductors who were always taxed as freelancers on all their income from each choir. We discussed the problem and agreed to seek advice from a chamber of barristers in the West End of London, '4 Pump Court'.

I presented a brief via a solicitor as per the rules at the time to the chambers. It showed how the accounts were split into various categories: choir rehearsal retainer, the performance fees, mileage for each, and a general description of the business undertaken as well as guest fees. The clerk to the chambers allocated our case to a young barrister who had recently started what would become a successful career, Mr David Milne, Q.C. He accepted the brief and I duly approached the tax inspector with a notice of the appeal, in which we specified it should be heard before the Special Commissioners for income tax. In those days this was the normal practice to be followed.

The Clerk to the Commissioners made arrangements for the case of *Kibblewhite v. CIR* to be heard at the Revenue's courtrooms in High Holborn. David Milne, his clerk, the Inland Revenue's solicitor and the two presiding Commissioners, along with Mr Kibblewhite and myself, all convened in this rather large empty courtroom. There was also another man, yet one more solicitor, who acted as a go-between for the plaintiff and the Q.C. All of the arrangements with '4 Pump Court' had to be made through him. In those days plaintiffs and their accountants were not allowed to deal directly with the barristers.

After Mr Milne had put his case, the Revenue's solicitor responded and cited various earlier tax cases of which none of us had ever heard. Mr Milne scurried back to his office in the coffee interval and again in the lunch break to examine the cases and then in the afternoon session to explain to the Commissioners why they were quite irrelevant. As the afternoon drew on the Revenue's solicitor continued to find more and more suspiciously irrelevant cases to counter our barrister's arguments.

Our solicitor had said that the procedure should only take one day but we continued through the second day. Mr Milne magnanimously agreed to our solicitor being dismissed to help us to save our costs and we never saw him after that first day. Moreover, Mr Kibblewhite had already returned to work on his choir engagements after the first morning. He was quite bewildered by how complex his affairs could be to the leading tax authorities!

At the end of the second day Mr Milne's parting words to me were that his perception was that the Commissioners were not in harmony with each other.

It took several weeks for them to reach their decision, which they delivered on 1st February 1982 and it made strange reading. It was deemed that choirs were only required to account and pay for PAYE if they had a written constitution that formally declared that there was a Director of Music. Mr Milne had sought to persuade the Commissioners that Mr Kibblewhite was an office-holder where the constitution declared there was a Director of Music. None of the constitutions of Mr Kibblewhite's choirs mentioned performance fees, therefore these fees were held to be freelance performance fees and part of his guest conductor freelance activities with all relevant expenses allowed. It was further held that where the choir's constitution did not refer to having a Director of Music those rehearsal fees were also freelance.

David Milne had managed to split the two commissioners 'down the middle'. My solicitor surmised that his colleagues at '4 Pump Court' were similarly bemused at David Milne's achievement.

The Revenue did not appeal and my client and I were delighted. We split his accounts between employed Director of Music and his other freelance earnings and quickly settled the affairs up to date with the Revenue. Moreover, Mr Kibblewhite was able to claim the expenses that he had been paid as office-holder *per se* against his PAYE employment income. He also claimed just about all of his other costs, including the barrister's fees, in the freelance part of the next year's tax return and everyone was content. The defeated tax inspector did not challenge this treatment.

We were now obliged to report the various P60 employment certificates in the tax returns as employments, by which those choirs should have set up PAYE schemes themselves. We also formulated the essential cost of employment allowable under the restrictive rules for Schedule E employments. Everything else was declared like a normal set of freelance accounts, with guest fees plus all the fees from choirs where there was no constitution requiring a Director of Music. It should have ensued that the Revenue needed to instruct each of the choirs which had a stipulated Director of Music in their constitution to set up a PAYE and National Insurance scheme for their one employee, Mr Kibblewhite.

Mr Kibblewhite and I were elated to realise later that none of the choirs with 'Director of Music' in their constitution were ever directed by the Inland Revenue to establish a PAYE scheme. Indeed, they never asked us for the address of each such choir. Neither Mr Kibblewhite nor I were keen to tell the honorary treasurers to await instructions from the PAYE office. Therefore no PAYE certificates were ever issued to Mr Kibblewhite for him to hand to me with his annual tax returns. However, in completing these tax returns I always put in the employment section the name of the choir with the words 'See P60' in the space provided for declaring gross and tax, which was the standard way of getting the Revenue to look it up for themselves. Indeed, in many cases the tax office clerks would 'prepopulate' their computer version of the tax return with the figures issued, and the Revenue would be alerted to looking up the P60 information from their own copies, known as P14s, and then enter them in the tax return if they had not already 'prepopulated' it in their computer version.

I told Michael that he should send me any P60 that arrived from any of the choirs. None ever came during the rest of his career. Michael and I were amazed that the Revenue ignored all of the hints that they should look up the absent figures on their copies of the P60s.

Meanwhile, not a single tax inspector in the next fourteen years ever noticed there were no P60s or P14s. Year after year unassessed employment tax and unpaid employment National Insurance mounted up in Michael's favour. It was only the nationwide switch to the self-assessment tax system that made it incumbent on an accountant and taxpayer to put the missing P60 figures in the tax return. After that time, 1996, Michael and I had to declare the figures that he worked out from those figures which would have been on P60 or P14 forms.

I was never contacted by any Revenue tax clerk over why Mr Kibblewhite wrote 'See P60' against the name of each so-called employer between 1982 and 1996. Quite often they misread the figures from the next taxpayer on their list. The system appeared to be designed to ensure that taxpayers did not get their entire annual personal allowance if there were more than one employment.

I was able to tell Mr Kibblewhite just how much he was not charged each year and I kept a running total for all fourteen years. However, I could not tell him how much National Insurance he, and the nominal 'employers', had not been charged. The huge savings for those fourteen years were certainly a hefty multiple of the costs of our taking the case to the Special Commissioners via the barrister.

In retrospect it is extraordinary to consider that the Inland Revenue did not pursue their victory in this part of Mr Kibblewhite's case, but he was very content with the outcome for all his freelance activity. During this time Michael had come to understand exactly what was going on and the incompetence of the Inland Revenue in their Commissioners' Office not handing down the implications of the Commissioners' decision. It was indeed a long battle but the achievement is quite unforgettable and we were both supremely delighted.

Every church organist is an employee by dint of his office. Vergers too are office-holders, but the Inland Revenue seems very reluctant to pursue parishes to operate PAYE systems and to account for the verger's cottage as his benefit in kind.

I watched Tax Cases, the annual volume devoted to important decisions, where the taxpayer or the Revenue had taken each other to task but sadly *Kibblewhite v. CIR* never appeared in the 1982 volume. I only hope that today's accountants are as consistent as I was in pursuing this line in similar circumstances which are quite common for talented musicians.

Whenever I subsequently took on a client musician, who ran a community choir as its musical director, I told them that by the choirs' constitution and the ruling in this case they were strictly employees due to be paid under PAYE. Two of them said that they did not wish to cause a comeback if the Revenue enforced the ruling on the choir. One said that he wished to work directly by the ruling, so we named the choir on his tax return in the employment section with 'See P60's. The Revenue never followed it up in my remaining years of business.

After the Commissioner's ruling, I had visions of the Revenue writing to every community choir and parish council in the country and insisting on PAYE schemes for their musical directors, organists, vergers, sextons and other office-holders. As far as I am aware this never occurred. I feel that they had never initially thought through what might be the consequences of their winning that part of our case.

It had all been an interesting experience for Michael Kibblewhite and myself and a waste of time for everyone else. The great shame is that the Revenue never published the decision in the fourteen years when the rest of the country could have taken huge advantage of it.

In 1998 there was a new headmaster appointed at my old school, King's College, Taunton. I hadn't realised until after he had retired that his wife was Michael Kibblewhite's sister; it is a small world!

The Kibblewhite case was by no means an isolated example of the Revenue wasting its own time and that of the taxpayers, their advisers and accountants, on simple common sense matters. The worst example that came to my notice was the Excess Profits Duty of the years 1915 to 1921 inclusive. Its intention was reasonable. Extra tax was suddenly required for the First World War effort for which the Wartime Coalition Government hurriedly pushed through an Act of Parliament to surcharge all trades and professions. By carelessness they forgot to surcharge vocations. This proved to be possibly the most expensive legislative *gaucherie* of the early twentieth century. It led to a huge amount of time and fees being absorbed by all interested parties in contemplating "What is a vocation?" and "What is a profession?"

This first came to my notice when sitting one day in a partner's office at Longcrofts'. While he quickly dealt with a phone call, I glanced towards a complete set of leather-bound Tax Cases volumes. Volume12 appeared extraordinarily fat. I asked the reason and the partner explained the heated discussion about how to define a vocation. The debate had endured for most of the years from 1916 to 1919. He suggested that I take the volume away and browse through it for a few days. It was amazing to see the arguments put forward by expensive tax counsels and the detailed judgements set down by the presiding judges. One example was a case concerning a typical firm of Estate Agents, Auctioneers and Valuers. In a considerable number of pages of the volume it was conceded that there was no trade involved (i.e. buying and selling). The word 'vocation' was carefully dissected and compared to definitions in earlier decisions. Nonetheless there were still yet more cases and hours expended in and out of court until a conclusive definition was adjudged.

Eventually all income tax returns and associated documents

included the words 'trades, professions and vocations'. With the advent of self-assessment in 1996, however, the Revenue mopped up all three categories by using the single word 'business'.

The nation was relieved at the victory over Germany at the end of the First World War. At the same time all actors and musicians and other such talented self-employed people would also have rejoiced in their own victory over the Inland Revenue in establishing that they exercised a vocation if they were not employees.

In the mid1990s the majority of my freelance clients had already reached the peak of their profession or (as emphasised by Volume 12 of Tax Cases in the instances of such people as my numerous musicians and singers) vocation.

One could never say that my career was monotonous while it rode from one such highlight to another.

PART SIX

FORCED RETIREMENT

I N 1988 I first noticed a focal phenomenon with my eyes when I was outdoors gardening. I thought little of it at the time but in 1989 it was my optician in a routine eye test for spectacles who first suggested that I had glaucoma. However, at Croydon Mayday Hospital the eye surgeon who saw me, Helen Seward, denied it. The next year the same optician re-examined my eyes. Hearing of her rebuff he assured me he had 35 years' experience as an optician and that I definitely had glaucoma. Reluctantly Miss Seward saw me again and she said, "Well, maybe you do have glaucoma." She directed me to an inexperienced young doctor for laser treatment, which he administered to my right eye. Four years later in 1994 I suffered a detached retina in that same eye. This time I went to Torbay Hospital near Totnes, where the surgeon, Sarah Livesey, who examined it, bungled the next operation. It was the ninth she had performed that day. She had made it bleed and introduced strabismus. By 2001 that eye was very blind.

In that same year, one of her colleagues told me that I should be seen by the hospital's glaucoma expert, Colin Graham. He explained that a trabeculectomy needed to be performed on both eyes and carried out these operations over the next two months. While deterioration continued, loss of vision in my other eye was very slow. After a few years the hospital offered him early retirement which he accepted, notwithstanding there was no longer a glaucoma expert on the hospital staff. Another surgeon suggested I should see Mike Smith, the glaucoma expert at Wonford Hospital in Exeter. He tried some minor adjustments to curb the very slow loss of sight, but it was when I needed a cataract operation in this left eye that he suggested laser treatment for the glaucoma. I reminded him of my 1990 experience but he assured me that now, in 2013, laser treatment was far less pernicious than in 1990. Reluctantly, and against my better judgement while lying in the operating theatre, I agreed to let him perform this 'less pernicious' laser treatment. However, it was an utter failure. Immediately I was unable to read files and work and had to arrange for my colleague Raymond Benn to take on as many of my clients as would agree to transfer to him. Happily almost all of my clients did so.

However, I was by then 68 years old and had already given 44 years of service to my private clients. I found that I had sent them 12,500 annual fee notes. I sent him notes on each client who agreed to move to him and I was very relieved that with only half a dozen exceptions, everyone was content with the way he basically ran the business on the same principles and with the same procedures as I had shown him when he started taking my overflow of clients in 1983. Unlike myself, he had taken on some good staff and had been expanding his business steadily, and I was able to retire satisfied and gracefully. Occasionally they telephone me with queries about how I dealt with situations that seldom arise to enquire what solutions in my experience were available.

When my clients heard that I was retiring I received many letters of disappointment and much deeply expressed heartfelt gratitude. They added reminders passed on to them by other clients who were impressed by stories of my work for them. They knew that I had no hesitation in getting the Revenue to alter things when I had seen them done wrongly in principle. I was quite surprised to find that groups of clients happily discussed between themselves the way I had dealt with some of their more unusual situations!

I get great pleasure from being able to say that I never truly lost anybody's file in the 45 years from when I set up freelance till I closed down in 2014.

In my early years of practice I had always made a point of

meeting each of my clients personally but this soon became impossible. When I finally retired I had a great many clients whom I had not ever met in all of my time of working for them, which was anything up to 42 years. I found that I would recognise their voices on the telephone at once and I had memorised the structure of everyone's affairs but not the precise figures. Evidently my parents had both done a good job in the way they brought me up to respect and to help other people.

One thing that has surprised me is just how many of my clients had been awarded an entry in *Debrett's People of Today*. This volume lists details of people who are deemed to be distinguished and is published annually. In about 1985 I was telephoned *by Debrett's People of Today,* asking for suggestions of names. The editor described what the book set out to achieve and asked me to recommend any significant clients within certain parameters. I compiled a list over the next fortnight and gave them several names. It was many years before I discovered that it was the chairman of British Petroleum (BP) who had put my own name forward in the first place. The last time I looked into it I found that 28 of my clients were detailed therein. More have joined its pages by their own merit in later years.

Retirement has allowed me time to reflect on the good and the bad in my life. Compared with my parents who lived through both the First and the Second World Wars, my generation was fortunate to proceed through life with our nation relatively at peace.

I cared greatly for the City where I had worked for sixteen years. I was truly saddened by two particular bombings that were carried out by dissident Irish groups. One was the bomb behind the Commercial Union Insurance building in Leadenhall Street, Bishopsgate, which left the ancient Church of St Helens very badly cracked. Even more tragic was the bomb left in a van on the east side of Bishopsgate outside the church of St Ethelburger, on the morning of Saturday 24th April 1993. It was doubly significant in having been the building in which the renowned Victorian stained glass designer, Charles Eamer Kempe, 1837 1907, began his career. The bomb exploded, blowing the whole of the west front of the church straight through the back of his magnificent stained glass window.

These were among the very few incidents not prevented by the assiduous diligence of Government Communications Headquarters and MI6, organisations to which we are all indebted.

For many years I have kept a keen eye on the country's railway network. Perhaps this was because my mother, her father and his cousin were all proud of their work on the Great Western Railway over many decades. I am adamant that the pruning of the railways by the governments of the late 1950s and the 1960s was disastrous. Almost every road and motorway built in that period and later has led to a massive increase in road traffic. This increase must have exceeded the substantial growth in our population.

Nowadays there are many areas where we are needful of the reinstatement of some of our lost lines to alleviate this increase. The usual excuse for not undertaking such work is that there is no longer sufficient rolling stock on the network to provide the service. The operators of the re-privatised railways have extracted excessive sums in profits, but little has ever been reinvested in extra trains and the re-opening of routes in areas where the population has become substantial.

I stand convinced that Ernest Marples did more long-lasting damage to the British transport system than any other minister in my lifetime. Turning to private enterprise for the rebuilding of any rail project is now no option because nobody would again trust Governments not to appoint a person to interfere once more or subsequently to renationalise and even close reinstated routes.

Nearly all of Britain's railways were built by private enterprise in Victorian times and in 1948 were nationalised by the government. The railways had rationalised themselves into four major groups in 1923 after the government had failed to pay a commercial rate on commandeering them for the duration of the First World War. In 1962 Ernest Marples directed Dr Beeching to over-rationalise them without regard to future population growth, which was already known to be unstoppable. During my career I watched the expansion of every conurbation, such as Washington in Northumbria, without the reinstatement of passenger rail services or rapid transit tramways near their perimeter. In my view it has been short-sighted not to introduce railways to growing suburbs because of the traffic jams which the growing population exacerbates in city centres.

As an observer, I believe that the following points should have guided Dr Beeching's brief…

- An earlier government should have instituted a far-reaching plan to modernise our extensive Victorian rail network with regard to the need to channel more commuters away from roads and on to double-track railways which are only about eight metres wide compared with new arterial roads.
- The vast majority of level crossings would have been automated and some of those on busy tracks replaced by bridges.
- Steam should have been scrapped at least a dozen years earlier than it was.
- Overhead electrification should have been introduced.
- A new Severn Tunnel should be bored downstream of the 1886 one.
- Non-corridor trains could have been exported to needy parts of the world so that tickets could be sold on board our newer passenger trains. Hundreds of stations could then have been destaffed.
- The vast majority of stations for crew signing-on at rural railheads should have been closed and replaced by the larger motive power depots serving several branch lines. The economies of scale would have outweighed the cost of the first train of the day running empty to the railhead and the last train of the day running back empty to the motive depot.
- Underused parcel station facilities should have been

decommissioned and replaced earlier by British Road Services.

- Branch line ticket offices should have been reduced to peak services periods or in most cases closed altogether, with tickets being sold by one or two conductors on the train.

- Slow freight locomotives should have been replaced by diesel or electric ones to run at line speed. This would have enabled passenger trains to run faster when sharing the same tracks.

- Timetables should have been redrafted so that passengers joining from branch lines could reach London by 09.00 hrs, although no such line should need to open for passengers before 06.00 hrs.

- No branch line should shut down for the night until it has provided a connection from the first express train to leave London after 18.00 hrs.

- Although the concept of power boxes was not to be available for many years, it would have been appropriate to dismantle a great number of older signal boxes. They had proliferated at intervals of four miles or less, yet no longer controlled active sidings, freight yards and crossing loops.

A small team of perhaps 150 competent accountants and engineers could have been appointed to draw up new plans for the network and to retrain the displaced railwaymen.

They would have acquired the new disciplines of electrical engineering and the maintenance of modern installations. Some of the accountants would have been engaged solely to plan redundancy packages for displaced staff. Men and women could have been offered no overtime and no pay rises and a normal rail pension if they did not want to take redundancy and were unable to find new jobs.

I welcomed the reprivatisation in the 1990s. Not all rail

operators selected men with adequate railway experience to be their managing directors. Chris Green at Virgin Rail and Adrian Shooter at Chiltern Railways were the best I encountered in these critical years. Mark Hopwood was appointed far too late at First Great Western to avert what had become its previous six years of chaos. Chris Green appointed Brian Johnson as his prime planner and controller on Virgin Cross Country. Brian had mapped out the routes for long-distance services across Great Britain decades earlier when at British Rail, but was never allowed to initiate them full scale.

Sadly a pansophic Richard Bowker of the Strategic Rail Authority disallowed many of Brian Johnson's routes, such as the routes to Portsmouth and to Liverpool. Richard then made a hasty exit into the unknown from the British Rail network after it was too late to restore Brian's well-founded plans.

Chris and Brian were distraught that their Cross Country vision was condensed after years of trying to set it up, first with British Rail and then with the new rail operators before having the chance to prove its suitability. Chris had embraced Brian's enthusiasm for running hourly long-distance facilities under reprivatisation. However, Virgin Rail had to forgo the depot which they had specially built at Three Bridges near Haywards Heath for the Gatwick Airport 'tentacle' of his inspired Cross Country system. All of this was to have been the key to modernising rail travel away from the metropolis and throughout Britain.

In a well-planned bid for the 2006 Great Western franchise, Adrian Shooter appointed Ian Baxter as his guiding light. He was to head his bid company, the London & Western Railway.

I gladly took up the invitation to set out twenty Devon and Cornwall embellishments that he could consider putting into the bid. He brought his team to Totnes one evening but I let others talk for the informal Totnes Rail Transport Group. At the close of the meeting he addressed me from the far end of the table and asked in which company or branch of the rail industry I had gained all of my experience. I was delighted! I replied that I had no professional experience but that since the age of eleven I had studied the construction of rail timetables and the positioning of crossing loops, but because 'Beeching cuts' were in full swing at the time when I was leaving school I eschewed the railways and trained to be an accountant instead. I explained that I had latterly learned a great deal about current operating procedures from committed long-service railwaymen. They were justly proud of their jobs and apprehensive for the future of the industry. I could have added that when I left school British Rail was not looking for innovative accountants...but I had said enough! I attach more pride to Ian Baxter's perception and comment than to any of the praise that I had received at any time for my achievements in accountancy.

If the British Railways Board had established a government-funded planning hierarchy I might have applied for a job in it, but the condemnation of railways by Ernest Marples would have deterred any applicant like myself. On the other hand I certainly don't regret having instead adopted the career I have depicted in these pages. On reflection I believe that I would have been quite frustrated in the rail industry.

Sadly, I entrusted much of my taxed profits to a stockbroker, not knowing his firm was running a scam. I quickly found that I had a capital gains tax loss of £240,000. It was many years before I again trusted a stockbroker, but only with £36,000, which I soon found was worth only £9,000. Alas this was another scam but the Financial Services Authority was now alert to immoral stockbrokers and I was reimbursed £28,000 from this financial authority, the FSA. With the compensation from the body came a warning which advised me not to trust stockbrokers with freedom to invest in future.

Disregarding my early stock market losses, I was delighted to find how valuable my pension fund had become at retirement. I owe it to my mother for encouraging me at an early age to be moderate and provident. It was she who induced me to pay off the small mortgage as early as I could afford to do so and then exhorted me to set aside pension contributions. These received higher rate tax relief at the time and so I quickly amassed a large pension fund without noticing its growth.

Throughout my career there was a catchphrase 'safe as houses' and not without good reason. After most people bought a house it was not long before they aimed to modernise their kitchens and to create additional rooms in their lofts and other spaces. As soon as I could, I set about many changes to the house in Totnes. I actually spent more on these works than I had on buying it. This included putting in offices for my girlfriend and myself. Various previous owners may have paid higher rates of income tax so that they probably could not afford what we saw as appropriate structural and design improvements. My girlfriend was absolutely marvellous with her design concepts for the house and garden so it was fortuitous that we had even inherited the gardener.

When I began my career in the City of London everything was in pounds, shillings and pence, until 'Decimal Day' on 15th January 1971. Everyone had been used to pence being divided into ha'pennies, being half a penny, and farthings, being a quarter of a penny. However, the last farthings were minted in 1952 and if you wanted school milk delivered to your home through the holidays, you had to pay fourpence-three-farthings (one fiftieth of a pound) for each one-third-of-a-pint bottle. The very last item to be sold in farthings was the Oxo cube, which cost a penny-farthing until late in the 1950s.

In the 1960s we had no electrical apparatus in our offices other than the telephone. However, there were many ingenious mechanical contrivances for adding up and subtracting, with ten and a bit rows and ten columns of keys. They were operated by a number of ladies who did not mind keeping their nails short. Their room was known as the counting house. Visitors would be fascinated to see hands leaping up and down as the fingers rearranged the keys in less than a second. The constant clatter would sometimes be punctuated by annoyed exclamations. There was a short column with just the farthing, ha'penny and three-farthing keys. An extra key would grapple with the minus procedure. Most of the machines completely jammed if a minus sum exceeded all of the plus sums already fed into it. Unjamming the machine often fell to the omniscient counting-house supervisor. She was a matron of a woman who gave the surly impression that she had never made an error in her life and that she foresaw that these young ladies would never rise to higher duties. She would sit on a raised desk at one end of the counting house, waiting for the next young lady to raise her hand and say, "Please, miss, I've jammed my machine again!" These heavy machines could stay on a clerk's desk for years but there were lighter, more portable varieties with today's square of keys but a very limited calculating capacity, like £999.99½.

It always amazed me that human brains had long ago invented the telephone, fully interlocking electric railway signalling, phased traffic lights and magnificent circuitry for the colourful advertising displays around Piccadilly Circus and yet they could not devise an electric calculator that could simply add five and six, let alone multiply that by four, divide it by six, deduct eleven, and show the answer as a minus sum.

So it remained right into the 1960s. Until then the counting-house clerks sat supreme, heaving on the large levers on their machines in order to register the sum to be added, then pulling it just to clear the total and to let the machine emit a scroll of paper with the analysis of the total displayed.

After I had joined Touche Ross & Co. and was working on the stockbroking partnerships, the head of purchasing came to my desk one morning with a salesman who had been endeavouring to coax him to have the simplest of electronic calculators on trial for a fortnight. Of course I was deeply suspicious of this contrivance and had no time to spare, as Derek Chapman wanted me to finish the task in hand before he went to see the client after lunch. There was no way this thing could be programmed to check cross-casts and percentages and I quickly perceived that I would not save any time over my mental arithmetic and multiplication faculties.

Taking my eyes off my task to see what buttons I needed to press would be too risky and in any case the digits which lit up the answer foreshadowed the digits not being displayed, so one saw all ten digits in various degrees of intensity and one was supposed to read only the brightest row of digits to see what answer the machine was trying to show. This was the extent to which progress towards desk computers had reached in 1970.

The head of purchasing returned for my progress report the next day so I told him of my reservations. We agreed that this was a novelty and that we should not waste time with it. The second and third generations of these machines might well have different keyboards and display layouts, rendering our time with this first machine a total waste. He passed it to someone else and probably got a similar report.

By the time I left Touche Ross & Co., the second generation of machines had arrived and they were indeed laid out differently and were easier to read. A report arrived from the team that helped clients with their PAYE schemes, saying that they had seen a couple of tax inspectors with electronic calculators visiting a client. Their machines had a 'x38%' key on them, presumably to help in income tax calculations as 38% was a much-used rate at the time.

Work was less frantic at Mr Goldsmith's tax department, and here I was glad to master the third generation of electronic calculator. It came to be the norm for the rest of my career. Soon I worked up a great proficiency and was able to foresee the speedy demise of clients' counting houses.

Those of us working in Cavenhams Foods Ltd tax department in Leadenhall Street included two secretaries, the junior of whom was Jenny. She was very reliable, accurate, focused and young. We did not really need a second typist but Mr Richards thought it sensible to pass the work which was more confidential to his senior secretary. On reflection I think this was wise. Anyway, these two were given very modern electric typewriters under a servicing contract. One day the servicing engineer turned up, disabled Jenny's typewriter and declared it to be irreparable. By the time Jenny had protested to Helen, the senior typist, that there was nothing wrong with her machine and Helen had conveyed the situation to Mr Richards, the engineer had left the building with a typewriter purchase requisite signed by the office manager who was in a different department. It made me realise that with servicing contracts come situations that you do not expect. Jenny's new typewriter arrived the next day and we were all the wiser. It was probably a ploy perpetrated throughout the machine company's customers.

At my home my father had bought me a cheap typewriter as a present in 1965. I used this until the carriage return lever fractured at a flaw in about 1976. I then bought a stouter machine which started to wear out in 1991. I rang for a service engineer. He had just happened to buy all of the Olivetti Linea 98 typewriters which were being trashed by a south London hospital trust. I knew that these strong machines were quite the best of mechanical typewriters and he sold me one for £45 fully serviced. It was built like a tank, never needed servicing again, and served me for the remaining 23 years of my career. Through the 1980s and into the 1990s the machine would regularly produce an average of 100 letters per week. I uphold it as the best investment in my business. I had bought it two gross of red and blue ribbons and never had a concern. I was often mocked by my clients for remaining mechanical but I took great comfort in hearing of all the failures of their computers, any one of which could have disrupted my business were I not trusting my Olivetti Linea 98 and its ceaseless production of 'carbon copies' which I would carefully file immediately.

I did hear about wonderful computer systems for accountants but found all of the descriptions confusing. Then one day a 'Letter to the Editor' in our professional press told of a client who had realised that computer science was evolving by leaps and bounds. He had taken out a two-year lease with an option to have the next generation of computer from this firm. However, they perceived a better system elsewhere and so did not exercise the option. On the day that the two-year agreement expired the system crashed. They had lost their entire client filing barring a few random papers where they had made hard copies. The firm was ruined overnight. Close reading of the original contract agreement proved that they did not have a leg to stand on. Many of my own clients found their systems crashing and in need of a computer engineer to get it all going again. Firms and clients were held up and unable to do any work for hours and in a few cases days. Even tax offices would tell me that they could not answer my queries because their system was 'down'. Yes, I was firmly deterred from computers and can frankly say that I have never lost an hour trying to find a file or waiting for an engineer. No wonder I was able to take on so many clients and to give a one-to-one personal service for 44 years.

My girlfriend gave me her Amstrad word processor in 1998, which she had bought in 1983 and updated. Using it, I spent four years thoroughly enjoying writing the history of my junior school and then five years preparing my book on rail operations. It certainly helped me to develop a fluent style of writing and gave me a huge satisfaction in doing research and correcting facts as I recalled my memories and observations. Very occasionally I used it for work but found it took me longer to use as I had perfected the ability to type on my Linea 98 without stopping to reflect on what I had written. It always bemused me that office partners whom I knew never typed their own letters. They would have saved themselves many secretarial costs if they had bothered to schedule their facts in the form of a letter and personally type it from memory, as was my wont.

In 1973 my employer, Cavenham Foods Ltd, provided free medical cover to its employees through the grandly named British United Provident Association, or BUPA for short. When I left the company in 1980 BUPA suggested I pay premiums for 'self and family' cover. I consented and paid as directed. Pre-existing medical conditions, in my case asthma, were understandably excluded, yet I was to have no trouble with asthma between the ages of 9 and 53. Nonetheless, BUPA tightened their rules on what they would pay out on, a ploy which recurred. Eventually when I did have trouble with glaucoma - the choice was to have the same surgeon perform the operations whether through BUPA or the free National Health Service. In the back of my mind there was always the fear that I might become too ill to work and need BUPA even on its ever-reducing benefits, so I faced the ever-increasing premiums until I retired. I then realised that the most recent premium cost more than an entire year's salary at the time I entered Cavenham Foods Ltd forty years earlier, and I gave up BUPA. Maybe in some areas of the country private medical insurance might have remained worthwhile but certainly not in Torbay where the National Health Service was well run.

Back in the City, I never wished to know which of my office colleagues consumed alcohol in the pubs at lunch time and again after work. Occasionally I accepted an invitation to somebody's party and took a glass of cider for the sake of politeness. After leaving the City in 1980 I have had no taste for beers, ales and spirits and have abhorred alcohol.

Many of my colleagues had girlfriends, or wives and even children who waited for their breadwinner to come home from the pub. Supper could be roasted to a cinder and the young children just about to fall asleep, or already in bed, deprived yet again of a family evening at home or out at a theatre or such.

Looking back I recall that unlike Mr Bunker's clerk's office, Mr Calver-Jones' clerks weren't in his adjacent room in earshot, so he had fewer clerks undertaking more work. I had learned the lesson never to have an office full of clerks and resolved to restrict the size of my business to what I could handle on my own. That meant I needed a large house so that I could shut myself up at one end, beavering away without non-client interruptions. With no high rates, rent, staffing, staff training and other office overheads, I am sure I made huge profits compared with Mr Bunker and Mr Calver-Jones, whose take-home cash must have been minuscule.

As I have already recounted, it was not until I had reached

the age of 22 that James Calver-Jones at Longcrofts' introduced me to the intricacies of personal taxation. I soon settled into something where I could, and indeed did, achieve excellence. My next personal inspiration was the writing, between 2002 and 2007, of a detailed history of the junior school at King's College. After four and a half years of work I published my first major book, *A Prep School in Somerset, the story of the Junior School of KING'S COLLEGE, TAUNTON to 1982.* The comprehensive five-hundred-page hardback book was compiled and edited to include memories of a broad selection of former pupils and teachers. The school had been founded in 1522 by Bishop Fox of Winchester as a memorial to his esteemed colleague Bishop Oldham of Exeter, a man who had endowed several educational institutions until his death in 1519. After difficult years the school was revived by William Tuckwell in 1864 and moved to substantial Victorian Gothic buildings. These were purpose built as a munificent gesture by Lord Taunton on what was then the edge of the town and on the site of the old Taunton racecourse which had marked the edge of town.

I also began to assemble the material for my second book, *Rail Operations Viewed from South Devon,* which I wrote between the ages of 62 and 67. I was comforted to have been assured that with both these books I had achieved excellence.

In 2017 it is still in preparation for publication.

After the 1950s it seems for a few decades we began to lose our appreciation for heritage buildings. John Betjeman was one of the most influential figures in the nation and he argued for the conservation of several of our significant old buildings. After the tragic demolition of the great Euston Arch and the public outcry that ensued he was influential in persuading the authorities to preserve St Pancras Station and Railway Hotel. These are some of the finest of George Gilbert Scott's creations. He was also the architect for the Prudential Assurance building in High Holborn in London. Thankfully authorities around the country are now more conscious of other great Victorian-era buildings such as the

Curzon Street Station in Birmingham designed by Philip Hardwick and built in 1838. Now that the railway is centred elsewhere, every plan for an alternative use of this building in Birmingham has so far floundered. For example, it was at one stage going to be the British Organ Archive with essays on the history of several significant organs and their builders as well as its own 46-stop concert organ. This idea is one of several that have died in their early stages.

Successive administrations have been placing many infrastructure contracts, such as the building and maintaining of trains and the rail network, in the hands of foreign companies. This has to be to the detriment of this country's manufacturers who had been quite capable of executing these contracts. Also it is preferable to employ British people if they are looking for the work, and can then pay their British taxes. I would welcome the idea of trained accountants going abroad to improve foreign professional standards and replacing them in this country with would-be accountants from abroad keen on gaining experience here for later use in their own economies.

This should keep our own economy more alive than it has been for decades. It all leaves this once great nation to be the laughing stock of wiser governments in our world. However, the reprivatisation of British railways has proved to be a success, in that the independent operators run far more trains at convenient times which significantly reduces road traffic. There is a trend to run trains at the same minutes past each hour such that timetables are easy to learn and time is saved in making enquiries. Somebody can plan a day's work from a memorised 'clock-face' timetable and decide to leave the car at their local station or even walk to it. Work can be done on their laptop on the train, which was not possible twenty years ago. Unfortunately, on arriving at city stations one finds the buses no longer have route boards such that it is a disconcerting task to have to enquire which bus goes along a particular route to one's destination.

Bus operators complain that nobody uses their buses so the

solution is to reintroduce the route board on the front and back of the bus. I have often driven around towns following buses that do not show their route, destination, and number. All drivers would benefit from knowing a few bus routes so that in future they could get around town without driving, trying to park their cars, or hailing a taxi. The immediate result of buses keeping secret their destination, route and number is that even the local population cannot learn the information such that routes and frequency are curtailed for want of passengers. Another problem with identifying bus services is the demise of the silkscreen-printed bus blinds in favour of electronic ones which change every few seconds while being read, especially when the front of the bus is not visible behind oncoming traffic to a prospective passenger at a bus stop. Another problem is buses going past stops where people wish to board if nobody aboard has asked the driver to stop; buses frequently pass stops when the prospective passenger has been given no chance to read its service provision. There is a very firm cult of bus designers and operators not knowing how to advertise the route, etc. on the back and front of each bus, and until they re-examine the clarity with which people could catch buses sixty years ago we will be in a negative financial situation with them. In about 1999 John Prescott made an announcement that government money was being directed into silkscreen-printed blinds with adequate route information such that most of this financial provision has been frozen or withdrawn.

Nonetheless, for the last seven years of my career I found that it was not necessary to commute to London at all as my work could be done from my desk at home in Totnes. All the work came and went by post which was reliable. Until about 1996 we had two postal deliveries daily. One could arrive by 07:00 hrs, or certainly by 08:30 hrs, and the second at around 11.30 hrs. Sadly the 11.30 hrs delivery was withdrawn and within a dozen years the early delivery ended and currently our post arrives at any time before 13.30 hrs. The once good system is still tolerable. Every increase in postal rates has been hailed as necessary for improvements or modernisation but the evidence highlights a heavily reduced service.

At the time of my final move to Totnes in 1993, I brought Ian Lowson's great wooden carved frieze down to my new office. I asked a local woodcarver, Bill Titley, to give it a good clean, replace a diadem that was lost from the king's crown and try to identify what it all depicted. Bill asked an expert friend to examine it and he suggested that it depicted the burning at the stake of the King of Alba, surrounded by many terrified Albigensians in 1209. The leader on the far left, who was mounted on horseback, was Simon de Montfort's grandfather, also named Simon. Neptune represents the English Channel. The figure sitting on the throne at the right with his bare left foot dangling over the steps of his throne is Pope Innocent III, on behalf of whom Simon de Montfort was leading this crusade designed to eliminate the Albigensians, who were deemed by the Roman Catholic faith to be descendants of Mary Magdalene. In the event the King of Alba escaped with his life and the crusade was apparently a waste of time. This is a great tenet of the Catholic Church.

The wood was now identified as neither oak nor mahogany but iroko, also known as African walnut. He confirmed that it was complete in its 2,750 square inches. Recent examination suggests that it is more likely to be a twentieth century Italian replica. Whether the Greek shipping magnate was right to bring the piece over to England is arguable, but as it was exported before 1938 there can be no problem about it staying. I paid the scoutmaster £1.50 for fetching it from Estates House with me. The frieze is the only memento that I received and have kept from any of the companies of the City for whom I worked. I am rather pleased to have been given a chance to own such a remarkable piece of craftsmanship.

Retirement has afforded me time to reflect on those persons who have enabled me to achieve what I did.

First of all are the contributions by my parents between the ages of 1 and 4½. Of utmost importance is ensuring an infant has no fear of water, by taking it, or get it taken, to the local swimming baths as early as possible to learn to swim various strokes. Sadly my parents both failed in this. I do not think either of them owned a swimsuit. Moreover, parents have a duty to socialise their children before school age, and it was not until I was age 4 that we moved to a housing estate in Cardiff where it was quite safe for all the neighbourhood children to play in the roads without supervision. However, my mother had engaged a young girl as carer for a few hours a day in business hours and she encouraged me to learn and write the alphabet, then spell and read simple words at our previous address which was on the busy A469 road.

My father played no part in my development as he had been adversely affected by a chemical experiment while in the Royal Engineers in 1940 or 1941. I was sent to the junior school of King's College Taunton, and what a wonderful environment it was. We were out in the woods climbing trees and digging dens all day Sundays and two afternoons a week. Pickaxes were wisely banned but many parents loaned shovels. Andrew Shawyer, the headmaster and superb Latin teacher, would come on the Great West Lawn to help supervise the rough game British Bulldogs three Sunday mornings a term and ensure that none of us got hurt. We always wore dungarees over our rugby shirts for these other pastimes. At 13½ I made the transition to the senior school. This senior school lacked the woodlands of the junior school and also half-holiday and Sunday activities when we were seldom allowed to go home. We were often bored, stuck in our common rooms without the television sets of today. These shortcomings were not unusual in similar schools of the era. The headmaster, Randall Unmack, was very strict with the staff of whom there were no more than one per form. Again, this was not unusual in those days as the governments had for years been threatening to 'close all public schools' without considering the consequences. It was to be many years before they realised it was better to work with these independent schools than against them.

In retirement I have come to realise that throughout my

life I have always aspired to excellence. This has been entirely subconscious, for one needs to have pride in tasks if one is to achieve quality and to achieve jobs without stress. Some pupil colleagues at school achieved merit in art through talent, not tuition. At King's College we had a rather good art teacher, William Lyons-Wilson, who taught the over-13s but only on Saturdays. He was a highly esteemed artist resident in Mousehole, Cornwall and would travel to teach at Blundell's School in Tiverton on Fridays and move on to King's College Taunton to teach on Saturdays. His lectures on art on Saturday mornings were well illustrated and informative but frankly the school would have been better served if the headmaster had employed a full-time art teacher to develop an art department for A-level students.

Unfortunately, hardly any pupil excelled in languages, because all of the lessons were in English not in the foreign language. In languages I achieved A-levels passes in French and Spanish but could never converse in them. I came to regret I had not been taught French in French or German in German lessons. The school academic curriculum was restricted to GCE O-level subjects, none of which was an inspiration to me other than maths. I also achieved A-level in Economics, which sadly in those days did not embrace Business Studies. How we might have benefited from visiting staff who could have come and enthused us! They could have taught us in voluntary Business Studies lessons and other subjects unheard of in those days, such as self-defence and a few more sports. There were only 12 sports at the school; the same school now has 33 for teenage boys and girls.

I would have excelled at essay writing if only we were encouraged to write more. Unfortunately, there was only one member of staff per class and no one to read and comment critically on one's essays. I appreciate that at Llandaff Cathedral Preparatory School the English teacher had taught detailed construction of adjectival clauses and adverbial phrases but I also resented being denied a wide vocabulary of nouns, adjectives and verbs at both King's junior and senior schools. It is apparent to me that while there are many new technical words entering the English language there is an end in sight of such words in prose as 'adumbrate, expiate, inveigle, inveigh'. Even 'inure, jocose and eschew' have become rare, as few people now know what they mean, while 'whom' seems no longer taught and is frequently misused. Listening to school pupils today I perceive that there has been a significant deterioration in the way English is taught. In many schools teachers have become very remiss in allowing pupils to utter split infinitives and interject phrases like "You know", "Like" and "An'en" which apparently means "and then" into their everyday speech. I know of one mathematics teacher in a comprehensive school who had a row with the English teacher over the standard of English that the pupils were bringing to his maths lessons. He resigned his post and has become a self-employed column writer in a railway journal, where he has earned huge respect for his detailed understanding of railway operations. British Broadcasting presenters have also begun splitting infinitives and unnecessarily ending sentences with a preposition such as was frowned upon by English teachers of two generations ago.

Latin was taught really well at both King's schools but History was a list of dates up to age 13 and then, when events should have been taught, we were faced with a master who would say "Um" as many as eleven times each minute; this I found to be highly distracting and I lost all interest although I knew he was hugely knowledgeable and well read. Science was not taught in prep schools as a rule and in my senior school the Chemistry teacher would only teach the brightest 30% of his pupils and leave the classroom for about 40% of the time rather than get the rest of the class through the O-level exam. The Physics master was quite the opposite, a great enthusiast who never had a failure at O-level.

Greek was an optional subject and did not begin until age 13½. I very much regret not studying it as I have always found my English vocabulary inhibited by ignorance of words derived from ancient Greek.

I found it easy to learn Mathematics from teachers in all three schools. They were enthusiasts and effective. Geography was very poor at both prep schools but happily I spent hours of holiday time poring over Great Western Railway maps and timetables. Thus I quickly learnt the whereabouts of all towns and villages with a halt in the vast Great Western Empire on its 1925 map issued to all its depot and station foremen such as my grandfather, who passed his old copies to me 1958. When the question had arisen as to what career I would adopt on leaving school it was generally expected that I would join British Railways. However, I had already realised that the network was too large to be viable any longer and that even where diesel trains had been introduced the timetables were still steam timetables, which had dwindled almost to nothing. I could not face working for so inefficient an organisation, and if the British Railway Board had done next to nothing, for instance, to design automatic level crossings, delete little-used or unnecessary crossing loops on single-lines, postponing electrification of all mainlines and so on, what chance would I have of coming in as a 19-year-old to implement many of the ideas that I had figured out in my leisure time? So I eschewed the railways for the next 34 years until I started to assemble material for my railway book, which I wrote between the ages of 62 and 67.

Puberty used to be a time to learn self-esteem, but now it is seen as an opportunity to have 'a jolly good time' amongst one's peers. Mr Unmack had a remarkable perception as to which boys had been told the facts of life, and would often figure out which boys needed talks where parents were shy, but he would not round up groups of boys for evening talks in his study without parental permission. My father, not wishing to admit to shyness, claimed he had told me everything, so I missed out badly and was left with obvious confusion about what girlfriends expected. I do wish Mr Unmack had spoken to my mother and then I would not have been such a late starter.

So I realised just how grateful I was to my mother for getting me a carer to teach me a few rudiments at ages 3 and 4, for sending me to be independently educated at Llandaff from age 4½, King's

Prep from 11 and King's College from 13½, helping me into an accountancy firm able to give me a thorough grounding in the accountancy profession at age 18½, and then, after I qualified, urging me to start serious tax-saving contributions to private annuities and pensions as soon as I had paid off much of the mortgage she had urged me to arrange at age 25.

Of course, my headmasters, Norman Westbury-Jones, Andrew Shawyer and Randall Unmack, were just as crucial and in the City John Palmer, James Calver-Jones and Derek Chapman were so crucial to preparing me for the stress-free career that I enjoyed. I hope they are generally proud of what I have achieved and I hope I have been helpful in reflecting the respect that people have shown to me.

Sadly, my father Thomas passed away in 1984 in Warlingham, Surrey and my mother, Ruby, in Dawlish, Devon in 1995, but not before I had taken her back at the age of 86 to the former site of the signal box at Exeter St Thomas' station where I had gestated while she was working as signaller in 1945. It was so pleasing to hear that she would recall her war-time railway career to her colleagues in the care home in which she spent the last months of her life.

By working on my own and saving office costs I avoided what I would expect to have been much frustration and time-wasting, especially if I had taken my own previous ineptitude as an employed clerk in the 1960s as a benchmark!

It is so important in life to have a stress-free career and this, thank heavens, is what I have had. Saying farewell because of increased blindness has been far from easy, but the most comforting thing are the fruits of my mother's pension advice in having a large lump sum and an unexpectedly high pension for the rest of my life. Recently this has enabled me to donate sufficient money for a granite-built amphitheatre and large extension to the art block at my old school, King's College Taunton.